PORTRAIT OF RILKE

PORTRAIT OF RILKE

An Illustrated Biography

Hans Egon Holthusen

Translated by W. H. Hargreaves

HERDER AND HERDER

1971
HERDER AND HERDER NEW YORK
232 Madison Avenue, New York 10016

Original edition: *Rainer Maria Rilke,*
in Selbstzeugnissen und Bilddokumenten,
© 1958 by Rowohlt Taschenbuch Verlag, GmbH, Hamburg.

CONTENTS

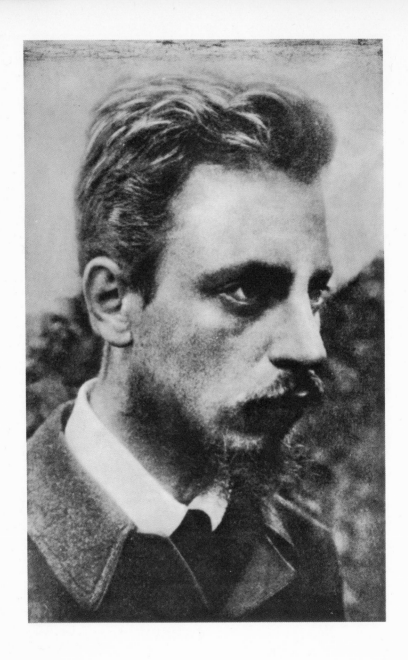

ANCESTRY AND PARENTAL HOME

RILKE was born in Prague on December 4, 1875; he was the only son of a marriage that had not proved very happy, and at his baptism six days before Christmas he received the names René Karl Wilhelm Johann Josef Maria. His father Josef Rilke had been born in 1838, the son of a steward in Schwabitz in Bohemia. He held the post of minor official with the Turnau, Kralup, and Prague Railway Company, and later tried to make the army his career. Although he had taken part in the Italian campaign of 1859 with the hope of receiving a commission and even held the post of commandant of the fortress of Brescia for a short time, he had soon been obliged to leave the service because of a throat problem. He retired to a dull civilian job that never gave him any satisfaction, and he was left with a sense of having been a failure in life. For even that employment had been obtained only with the help of a successful and influential brother, the district advocate and member of the provincial diet, Jaroslaw Rilke, who was raised in 1873 to the hereditary nobility with a coat of arms, a motto, and the title of Rilke, Ritter of Rüliken.

The mother, Sophie or Phia Rilke, born in 1851, was a difficult and arrogant but not untalented woman from the upper middle class. She was the daughter of the merchant and Imperial Councillor Carl Entz and his lovely and vivacious wife Caroline who was almost a centenarian when she died in 1927. Rilke's mother had grown up in an imposing baroque palace in the Herrengasse in Prague, and her marriage in 1873 to a disabled officer was and remained a mésalliance. She lived in a world of make-believe, dreaming of social successes which her husband

7

Entrance to the Rilke house.

was unable to procure for her; she raved about the nobility and high society and liked most to dress in black after the manner of widowed archduchesses. She followed the taste of her times in interpreting her fate as that of a disappointed and emancipated woman; a small volume of aphorisms which she had printed in the proud year 1900 under the title *Ephemeriden* is evidence of an unsatisfied hunger for life and a kind of yearning skepticism. After scarcely eleven years her marriage had already broken up; since 1884 she had been separated from her husband and living chiefly in Vienna so as to be near the court. She survived Josef Rilke by a quarter of a century and even her famous son by nearly five years, her own death coming in 1931.

Subsequently, of course, this son more than managed in his own way to satisfy the tortured ambition of his mother, and by his rise to artistic fame he also surpassed the boldest of those expectations which had remained unfulfilled in her own life. Many names from the most eminent noble families of Europe figure among his correspondents; to be sought after as the admired guest in palaces and in the highest circles was a matter

Rilke's parents.

of course. He came and went as he pleased and was moved only by the absolute subjectivity of his inmost needs; he needed high society in order to procure for himself a temporary domicile and good conditions in which he could work, but he never failed to leave again as soon as he came to believe that his "solitude" was threatened. He was the favorite of a social order which just then and perhaps for the last time could make possible a way of life such as his, with its complete (subjective) detachment from society, before it collapsed under the violent shocks of that age of world wars: an order which already had within itself a deep feeling of man's loneliness and forsakenness in the anonymity of large towns, yet still allowed an upper class to cultivate its taste in aesthetic matters; it was a world of hotel rooms and houses of the nobility.

In Rilke's relationship to the aristocracy there can be seen the naïve snobbery of his mother, on the one hand intensified but on the other spiritualized as well and overcome by an extreme need for independence. Where he examines his social situation, he is in essential agreement with certain favorite notions of his times as they are to be found in *fin de siècle* literature from Hofmannsthal to Thomas Mann: the artist is a refined and solitary latecomer, the last of an old and aristocratic race whose final, sublime flowering he represents. In this sense he stylized his descent and insisted for a long time that he himself came from an old noble family which could trace its origins back to Carinthia and the thirteenth century. According to this tradition which was fostered artificially, a branch of the family had moved to Saxony towards the end of the fifteenth century and from there many of its members had subsequently emigrated to Bohemia. Although the three-year genealogical search which Jaroslaw had once set in train had been unable to establish any connection whatsoever between his family and the Carinthian and Saxon nobility, the beautiful illusion was nevertheless stubbornly preserved by Mother Phia and implanted forever in her son's memory:

> The old, long-noble race's unregressing
> distinction in the eyebrows' archingness—

these are the lines we find in a lyrical self-portrait written in 1906, which is contained in the first part of *New Poems*. "Portrait of My Father as a Young Man," a verse sequence dating approximately from the same period, the year of Josef Rilke's death, seeks to detect the flattering features of the aristocratic in the figure of the father, this rather petty bourgeois faint-heart both in profession and marriage. But in this case praise is bestowed on the penultimate phase before the artistic sublimation, namely, on the military bearing which was still self-assured but had already grown weary and frail.

But at times Rilke himself relegated his aristocratic descent to the realm of legend. It was an invention of his poetic imagination and as such can be credited with a higher, symbolic truth which must not necessarily agree with historical facts. It was not caprice and it had nothing to do with silly fraud if the poet in *Notebooks of Malte Laurids Brigge* (1910), a kind of imaginary autobiography in mirror writing and intended to be read "against the stream," shifted the scene of his hero's childhood to an aristocratic world which to an impossible degree was peculiarly sensitive, over-refined, and introspective and to a Denmark full of ghosts and Nordic melancholy. These themes stem from his innermost being: his thoughts, resembling leitmotif's, could only be developed under such atmospheric conditions.

Concerning Rilke's childhood we possess abundant evidence, both poetic and epistolary, from his own hand. Scarcely any of it can be described as purely "autobiographical." Almost everything he wrote about this period has been involuntarily stylized and transformed by the imagination. "Childhood" was a cardinal

11

At age 2.

theme in his thinking and writing, and whatever he had to say
about his own childhood was not just direct experience but always
experience interpreted in the sense of his theme. To Rilke childhood was on the one hand "inwardness" and on the other
"anxiety," both of an extreme intensity which surpassed all later
capacity for experience.

"Inwardness" is the primordial oneness of the child with that
which the poet calls "nature," with the sustaining, growing, giving forces of being, it is the most inward of the human capacity
to feel, which is alike in substance to the inexhaustible fullness
of nature and is experienced as a "heavenly" gift of grace. But

inwardness is only the reverse side of anxiety, and the child's protectedness can only be measured by his defenselessness:

Not that it's harmless. The petting and prettifying error
that be-aprons it and be-frills
it is no more certain than we and never more shielded;
no god can counterbalance its weight. Defenseless
as we ourselves, defenseless as beasts in winter.
More defenseless—no hiding places. Defenseless
as though itself were the thing that threatened. Defenseless
as fire, giants, poison, as goings-on
at night in suspected houses with bolted doors.
For who can fail to see that the guardian hands
lie, while trying to defend it, —themselves in danger? Who may
     then?

To the question asked here the following reply is given:

"I!"
—What I?
"I, mother, I may. I was fore-world.
Earth has confided to me what she does with the seed
to keep it intact. Those intimate evenings! We rained
Earth and I, softly and Aprilly, into the womb.
O male, who shall make you believe in the pregnant concord
we felt together? For you no annunciation
of cosmic peace concluded round something growing! . . ."
Maternal magnanimity! Call of the comforters. Yet,
what you've described is peril itself, the entire
pure perilousness of the world,—and thus it turns to protection,
soon as you feel it completely. Then fervour of childhood
stands like a center within it: out-fearing it, fearless.

Earth, nature, mother, womb: those are the values which are here set against the predominance of man and father in the traditional conviction of European culture. They signify a thematic center of emphasis in the poet's work, not the only one and perhaps not the most important, but one which must have been formed at an early date and then received more and more stress in the course of his artistic development. Inwardness comes increasingly to mean a purely "natural" bodily-sexual awareness; a kind of mysticism of the womb seeks to find expression in numerous passages in his later work.

What Rilke has to say about his own mother often forms a striking contradiction to the divine, maternal image in the quoted fragment. When he was nineteen years old, he did not shrink from calling her a pleasure-seeking, contemptible creature in a letter to the first woman who was his friend. At the age of twenty-two, he told with deep melancholy of a friendly old peasant woman whom he met hay-making in a meadow near Wolfratshausen and then went on: ". . . and later I thought: would that I had a mother as simple and as happy and God-fearing to the very core in her work as was this old woman . . ." (to Lou Andreas-Salomé, September 8th, 1897).

Just as he can be quite unreflecting and positive in his relations with women in general, quite ecstatic and exaggerated in his choice of words, so he can become quite inexorably harsh and cutting when his mother of all persons trespasses on his solitude and threatens by a single, grotesque misunderstanding to invade the monastic cell of his freedom.

A letter from Rome to Lou Andreas-Salomé on April 15, 1904, contains the following lines: "My mother came to Rome and she is still here. I only rarely see her but—as you know— every time I meet her I have a sort of relapse . . . Whenever I am obliged to see this lost, unreal, incoherent woman, who cannot grow old, I feel how as a child I tried to get away from her, and deep within me I fear that even after many years of wandering I am still not far enough away from her, and that somewhere inside me I still have emotions which are the other half of her withered gestures, broken fragments of memories which she carries about with her; then I shudder to think of her rambling piety, her headstrong faith, and all the twisted notions to which she has clung, herself as empty as a dress, ghostly and horrible. And that nevertheless I am her child; that some secret door in this isolated, shabby wall was my entry into the world—(if it may be said that such an entry can possibly lead into the world . . .)!"

In contrast to this uncompromising account of the break away from his mother, other texts can be quoted in which a passionately tender relationship between son and mother are described. The best known example is in *Malte Laurids Brigge:* it is the passage where the writer of the notes conjures up to himself the fears and deep feelings of his childhood: "Mother never came at night—or rather, she did come once. I had cried and cried,

Prague: the Hradschin and the Karlsbrücke.

and Mademoiselle had come and Sieversen, the housekeeper, and Georg, the coachman, but that had been of no avail. And then finally they had sent the carriage for my parents, who were at a great ball, at the Crown Prince's, I think. And all at once I heard the carriage driving into the courtyard, and I became quiet, sat up, and watched the door. There was a slight rustling in the adjoining rooms, and Mother came in in her magnificent court robe, of which she took no care—almost ran in, letting her white fur fall behind her, and took me in her bare arms. With an astonishment and enchantment I had never experienced before, I touched her hair, her small smooth face, the cool jewels in her ears, and the silk at the curve of her flower-scented shoulders. And we remained like this, weeping tenderly and kissing one another, until we felt that Father was there and that we must separate. "He has a high fever," I heard mother say timidly; and my father took my hand and felt my pulse. He wore the uniform of a Master-of-the-Hunt with its lovely, broad, watered blue ribbon of the Order of the Elephant. 'What nonsense to send for us!' he said, speaking into the room without looking at me. They had promised to go back if there was nothing serious the matter; and there certainly was nothing serious. But I found Mother's dance-card on the cover of my bed, and white camellias, which I had never seen before and which I laid on my eyes when I felt how cool they were."

This episode too, one is tempted to conjecture, cannot be pure "invention." Again, personal memories have undergone a poetic elaboration. Is it not more than probable that Phia Rilke, disappointed and unhappily married, could have lavished an excess of feeling on her only son? She spoiled and pampered him, until he was six years old she dressed him in girls' clothes, supposedly in order to be reminded of a daughter who had died at a very early age: this motif too, like many other authentically autobiographical details, has been used in *Malte Laurids Brigge*. Nevertheless, it would be an oversimplification to say, as has occasionally happened, that our poet suffered from a mother-image fixation. The contradictoriness in the attitude of this son to his mother is rather a particularly striking example of his complicated and broken relationship with any fellow human being as an object of love in general: there is at one and the same time surrender (due to deep feeling) and resistance (due to loneliness). The short story *Ewald Tragy* (1900), in which the twenty-year-old author writes about his departure from Prague for Munich, his loneliness in the strange city, and an illness and convalescence in a very slightly enciphered form, ends with a characteristic gesture: the hero writes a fervent letter to his mother but, instead of sending it, he destroys it.

During the whole of his life, Rilke treated the problem of his descent and also the portrait of his mother as a subject for poetic invention. Anyone who seeks for biographical truth in one or another interpretation along the lines of depth psychology will sooner or later encounter the right, the sovereign consciousness of the poetic imagination which deals with its recollections according to its own notion of truth. For the poet there is truth both in the intense tenderness of the *Malte Laurids Brigge* episode and in the dismay caused by his mother and her destructive invasion of his own "house," which was expressed in a poem dated 1915 in alarmingly striking words:

> Alas, my mother will demolish me!
> Stone after stone upon myself I'd lay,
> and stood already like a little house round which the day
> rolls boundlessly.
> Now mother's coming to demolish me:
>
> demolish me by simply being there.
> That building's going on she's unaware.
> Through my stone wall she passes heedlessly.
> Alas, my mother will demolish me!
>
> In lighter flight the birds encircle me.
> The strange dogs know already: this is *he*.

17

Junior Military School at Sankt Pölten.

It's hidden only from my mother's glance,
my gradually augmented countenance.

No warm wind ever blew to me from her.
She's not at home where breezes are astir.
In some heart-attic she is tucked away,
and Christ comes there to wash her every day.

The last two lines refer to the headstrong and bigoted piety of Phia Rilke from which the son moved away ever more passionately as he grew older, although once, as a child, his imagination had owed it an incalculable debt—it had meant for him lessons, myth and legend.

After spending his first years at the fashionable school of the Piarists in Prague, little Rilke was sent in September 1886 to the Junior Military Academy at Sankt Pölten where he remained until he was transferred in September 1890 to the Senior Military Academy at Mährisch-Weisskirchen. It had been decided that he should be an officer so as to occupy one day that social position which had been denied his father. These years spent in receiving a military education which was certainly not particularly imaginative remained later in the store of Rilke's memories

18

as nothing else but a "primer of horrors," a visitation beyond measure. True, he survived it with his soul intact, and it is even reported that his diligence and intelligence received recognition, that his particular gift was respected, and that he was even allowed to recite his earliest poems to the whole class. Nevertheless, in Rilke's eyes this period was one of brutal servitude and it always remained for him the primal model of that experience of suffering which was peculiarly his, a suffering that was unalloyed and boundless.

Rilke speaks of the daily despair of a ten-, twelve-, fourteen-year-old boy; with real bitterness he states that when he left school he was "exhausted, physically and spiritually violated." "But," he says, "even today I can recall how I clenched my teeth and found a sort of help in the fact that those foul and fearful years of my childhood had been so completely horrific, without the least mitigation." His use of the word "repression" seems to bring him close to the terminology of psychoanalysis, even if it was not consciously his intention to refer to it. In fact he did show interest in this new branch of learning and for a while, under the influence of Lou Andreas-Salomé, his beloved at the time when he was writing *The Book of Hours,* he considered having himself analyzed. But an unerring instinct for the originality of his life's work saved him from interpreting the burden of his childhood memories simply as "trauma," as can be seen from a letter to Lou dated September 9, 1914, in which he gives an account of a consultation he had with the specialist Dr. Freiherr von Stauffenberg in Munich: "I was horrified to feel sometimes a kind of mental nausea, which he endeavored to create; it would be dreadful to bring up portions of one's childhood like that, dreadful for someone who is not obliged to dissolve inside himself what still remains unsubdued, but is called upon in a very special sense to make full use of it, transformed, in what he invents and feels, in things, animals—is anything unsuitable?—if need be—in monsters."

19

Rilke had to refuse to resort to medicine for psychological relief. He considered it an obligation imposed upon his heart to endure, to outdo even that which was most dreadful and destructive and thereby to make it inwardly his own. That is the sense in which the remarkably conciliatory phrases in his letter to Major General von Sedlakowitz of the school should be understood: "When, in more meditative years (how late I came into the realm of books, reading them calmly and receptively instead of making up for lost time!) I first got hold of Dostoevski's *House of the Dead,* I would seem to have been initiated into all the terrors and despairs of prison from my tenth year! . . . To a child's mind, the prison walls of Sankt Pölten could assume roughly the same dimensions if it took as measuring rod its hopelessly forsaken heart.

"That is twenty years ago; then I stayed for some time in Russia. An understanding which had only been fostered in the most general terms by a reading of Dostoevski's works became incontestably clear to me in that country which was my spiritual home; it can be formulated only with difficulty. Something like this, perhaps: the Russian has shown me in so and so many instances how even an enslavement and a visitation that continually overwhelm all powers of resistance need not necessarily bring about a degeneration of the soul. There exists, at least in the soul of the Slav, a degree of submission which deserves the epithet perfect because even under the most massive and annihilating pressures it creates for the soul a secret arena, a fourth dimension in which, however grievous conditions become, a new, endless and genuinely independent freedom can now begin.

"Was it presumptuous for me to imagine that I had accomplished a similar absolute surrender, instinctively, in my earliest years, when a solid mass of misery was trundled over the tenderest shoots of my being? I had, it seems to me, some right (on a different scale, of course) to such an assumption since I cannot

20

point to any other means by which I could have survived that monstrous, over-life-size injustice.

"So you see, Herr General, that I long ago undertook to come to terms with my earlier fate. Since this fate did not destroy me it must, at one time or another, have been added as a weight to the scales of my life,—and the counterweights, which were destined to tip the balance, could only come from that purest achievement on which I found myself determined after my sojourn in Russia."

Rilke could endure life in Mährisch-Weisskirchen for only a few more months and then he had to leave on July 6, 1891, because of ill-health. The attempt to give him a military education had proved a failure. Later he said that for another year he was ill and too confused to know what to do. The unsuccessful cadet was sent off to Linz to attend a school of commerce, but in May 1892 he returned to Prague. Finally, Uncle Jaroslaw, who was energetic and indefatigable in promoting the family interests, stepped in and took steps to give a positive direction to his nephew's education. He gave him an allowance of 200 gulden a month to enable him to be coached intensively for the final secondary school examination and subsequently to study law. One day, he thought, young René would take over his law practice.

To begin with, his nephew did not disappoint him, although he had quite different ideas in his head. He worked hard for three years and took the examination at the Deutsches Staatsgymnasium in Prag-Neustadt and passed with distinction. At the beginning of the winter semester 1895/96 he matriculated at the Karl Ferdinand University in his native city. First of all he chose the philosophical faculty and attended lectures on philosophy, German literature, and art history, but six months later he changed to jurisprudence although he was not seriously interested. After another six months he had shaken off everything which might harass, confine, or keep him from his artistic studies:

21

at the end of September he had turned his back on Prague and settled in Munich, where he could devote himself exclusively to literature and the affairs of his restless heart.

Now that he had completely detached himself from his native country and his family, an unsettled life began with much travelling. In a letter dated December 30th to Xaver von Moos, a young Swiss, Rilke explained why he took this course: "When, in his time, my father expected me to pursue the art to which I thought myself destined, as a hobby (side by side with the career of officer or lawyer), it is true that I burst out into the most violent and persistent refusal: but that was entirely the fault of our position in Austria and the narrower milieu in which I grew up; a milieu, moreover, which was still so close to the sophistications of the '80's that it would have been utterly unthinkable to have accomplished anything real or resolute with one's strength divided; indeed, in order to begin at all, I had to detach myself altogether from the conditions of my home and country, counting myself among those who, only later, in the lands of their choice, might test the power and fertility of their blood."

THE MODEST BEGINNINGS
OF A DISTINGUISHED TALENT

WHEN Rilke moved to Munich, he was certainly not an author with nothing to his credit. On the contrary: at a very early, certainly a much too early date, he had begun to have his attempts at poetry printed; they were chiefly lyrics but there were also prose sketches, stories, and plays; between the early ages of nineteen and twenty-one he had quite inundated Prague literary circles with immature publications. No reader of Rilke who traces his activity back beyond the threshold of his artistic maturity which may be fixed in 1899 will discover without a feeling of dismay how trivial the early work of that poet was who went on to write the *Duino Elegies*. It would be hard to detect in the language and approach of young René convincing indications of future mastery. Hundreds of mediocre poems reveal nothing more then a poetaster's extraordinary facility, a lyrical loquacity which pours banal feelings into empty linguistic forms and scarcely ever rises above the level of the two-a-penny articles of those days. The prevailing Heine influence which for decades had dominated the taste of the reading public had not yet been overcome; the decadent members of the bourgeois from Gustav Falke to Martin Greif and Wilhelm Arent determined the thematic and stylistic canon, and the time had not yet come to break away from it. Although Hofmannsthal had already written things like *The Death of Titian* and *The Fool and Death* and was going on to write *The Little World-Theater*, Rilke, who was only a year younger, was still turning out romantic blood-and-thunder ballads and lines such as:

> Now when from night day brings release,
> and in Wolfsmoor all springs to life:
> today Count Eric shall seek peace
> with Jutta, his own lawful wife.

That, roughly, is how the poem "Attempt at Reconciliation" begins which was published in the *Deutsches Dichterheim* in 1895. A helmet flashes in the blue air, a stallion paws the ground, a golden litter is borne along, rhymes are forced—, until the whole tragic happening reaches its catastrophe in an involuntary comic concluding effect (in the German only):

> And fear comes o'er him, he knows not why.
> He shouts. —In vain! His eyes are red
> with rage. —At once the stallions shy,
> inside lies Countess Jutta—dead.

23

Her own sharp blade has ta'en her life.
The smell of blood affrights the steeds.
One rears. —And there beside his wife
with fractured skull Eric now bleeds.

In contrast to Hofmannsthal who had grown up in the refined atmosphere of the upper middle class, young Rilke had
to manage without the slightest elementary grounding in taste
and culture, and in contrast to George he did not enjoy the
company of distinguished artists who might have fully developed his gifts at an early age. As for the defects in his
education, he always said he was self-taught, and even as an
adult he considered taking a systematic course of study; a
certain unsureness in matters of taste was still noticeable even
in later years. His development also suffered from the general
poverty of literary life in his own native city. What the literary
historian Peter Demetz (who himself comes from Prague)
calls provincial backwardness when referring to the Prague
scene of the 90's did indeed give him the opportunity to appear
in public at a very early age, but on the other hand it prevented
his genius from developing rapidly. A feeling of ambitious esprit
de corps made him associate with local worthies whose names
have long since been forgotten; he sought their critical approval
and received it abundantly. Letters written during these years
show that he was much involved in the daily happenings in
literary circles, seeking stimulus from news of the moment,
chasing after contacts, relishing the still novel enjoyment of
seeing his work in print, experiencing the vanity and the
touchiness found in discussion circles, and last but not least learning about the minor sensations at the theater and among actors.
Later Rilke gave as the explanation for the almost embarrassing
activity at this stage in his life the fact that he had to show
himself in a successful light to his disapproving family; however,
an unbiased study of the sources which have just recently been
brought to light, especially in the book by Demetz, gives a

different picture. This man who later was to remain consistently aloof from all publicity in the literary world, almost to idolize his loneliness and acquire nearly legendary fame by pursuing his art with unswerving single-mindedness and austerity: at the age of twenty he behaved like a giddy-headed youth.

He supplied numerous newspapers and lesser reviews with frivolous contributions in prose and verse, he thrust himself and his products on poets who were travelling through Prague, he made good use of authoritative names, and in his conversations with publishers and editors he was like a man with ripe experience, showing a remarkable kind of childlike-insistent business capacity. He was frequently to be seen as an enthusiastic guest in two different German artists' clubs, but at the same time he was pursuing a plan to supplant and replace them both by founding a radical League of Modern Enemies of Pedantry. In a letter to Láska von Oesteren, a young lady who wrote articles and on whom he had cooly conferred the title of baroness, paying her his respects at great length, he expressed this idea in the following words:

> With dull and dreary pursuits bored,
> I'll try to make the city Prague
> A home of artists' toil.
>
> . . .
>
> All artists full of similar thoughts,
> Their minds quite centered on today,
> Who modern poems write.
> Whose gaze is upturned to the sun;
> They build their ardent bridges blue
> To every radiant star.

Near the end of the same letter (dated March 16th, 1896), there is a most characteristic remark: "Today I am enclosing one of the free copies of my venture 'Wegwarten' (a gift to the people). If it interests you, gracious baroness, I shall send you in a few days by book *Offering to the Lares* which has been received with loud applause. (Dr. Klaar reviewed it in yesterday's *Bohemia.*)"

Enthusiasm for the social cause is to be found here together with an uncritical founder's mania and the naïve self-confidence of the beginner who had often seen his work in print. "Wegwarten," a publication resembling a review, was printed by the author acting as his own publisher. It was to appear at fairly regular intervals once or twice yearly, being financed by benefactors and distributed free of charge to hospitals, artisans' clubs, and the like, but it ceased publication with the third number (October 19th, 1896). Other projects were: an Austrian edition of the review *Jung-Deutschland* and *Jung Elsass* in connection with which Rilke gave his Strassburg publisher Gottfried Ludwig Kattentidt a solemn promise to find a large number of Austrian subscribers; and in addition the foundation of a so-called intimate theater, which would open its doors to plays which for one reason or another had been condemned by the stage. Which author was to profit most from this free stage can be seen in a letter also addressed to the most gracious baroness: "I wish particularly to produce Maurice Maeterlinck from the Low Countries. Hermann Bahr in Vienna has of course written quite a lot in various places, including his excellent weekly *Die Zeit,* about Maeterlinck, and you will no doubt be aware of his characteristic style. M. has created the drama in which the souls alone have experiences. This is the drama whose most eloquent language is silence, whose catastrophe is 'screaming quiet.' "

Neither of the plans were ever realized.

René Rilke's enthusiasm for the theater, as we have said, led him mistakenly to experiment personally with dramatic subjects. For his first attempts he used the naturalistic manner (*Jetzt und in der Stunde unseres Absterbens, Im Frühling,* both dating from 1896), later he took the Symbolists as his models

26

(*Höhenluft,* 1897, *Ohne Gegenwart und Mütterchen,* both of which were written in 1898). As a dramatic subject the young poet found misery no less attractive than psychology, and he can be seen showing the same enthusiasm for both at once. The same letter in which admittedly there is praise for Maeterlinck, he prefers nonetheless a certain Rudolf Christoph Jenny and speaks admiringly of his excellent three act popular play *Not kennt kein Gebot* (*Necessity Knows No Law*), the first performance of which was to take place in Prague that same evening (May 6th, 1896). Jenny, who was seventeen years older than Rilke and respected by him as his dearest friend and master, was one of the closest circle of Prague companions. Born in Stuhlenweissburg, he had gone to Tirol as a child and, after a varied career as officer, actor, and author, had in later years come to Prague to study philosophy. His play, which made every concession to the characteristic trend in contemporary taste, was performed on several Austrian stages, including that of the Viennese Raimund Theater, with considerable success. It deals with the conflict between a poor family of tenants and a rich, unscrupulous landlord. Rilke was so impressed that in his *Absterben* he attempted to take up almost exactly the same theme. But he did not succeed in achieving the vigor and dialect-flavor of the popular play which was his model; the language of his dialogue is less colorful, more "literary," a lifeless attempt to transfer the style of Berlin naturalism to Prague. On August 6th, 1896, this melodramatic, coarsely sentimental, one act play was given at a benefit performance at the German Volkstheater in Prague. This event took place in a town which was deserted for the summer—"Prague is quite empty" the author wrote to Jenny in a letter dated midday, August 6th—and was not repeated, although mention was made of its "success." Almost a year later, on July 20th, 1897, Rilke's second dramatic attempt, *Im Frühfrost,* was produced at the

German Volkstheater. This time it was a Berlin company which staged the play. Among the actors was a young man named Max Reinhardt.

But even in this very early period the center of gravity in Rilke's output already lay in the field of the lyric. His first collection of poems appeared in 1894 under the title *Life and Songs*. It is dedicated to the niece of the Czech poet Julius Zeyer, Valerie von David-Rhonfeld, and its one theme is the love which bound the author to this pretty, dreamy, and poetically inclined girl who was a year older than himself. Rilke had met her in January 1893 and remained faithful to her until the summer of 1895. "All my life so far seems to lead to you," he wrote in a letter to her dated December 4th, 1894, his nineteenth birthday: "like a long, dark journey at the end of which my reward is to aspire to you and to know that you will be wholly mine in the near future." Vally was the first girl Rilke as a youth ever seriously loved, yet she belongs entirely to this very early period. This partnership is comparatively irrelevant for his spiritual and poetic development for the good reason that his individual life story, when his feelings and his writing had matured, had not yet begun, nor could his psyche yet cope with a woman of epoch-making stature. Vally certainly put more "fate" into the affair than did her poet; but a few melancholy notes which were written by her tell us nothing to justify the word "tragedy."

The volume *Life and Songs,* which could be printed only thanks to Vally's financial support, consists chiefly of variations on the theme "My love has stolen my heart away" and contains scarcely anything which goes beyond the horizon of the bourgeois ardor and the tentative aesthetics of a Gymnasium pupil. *Offering to the Lares* appeared at the end of 1895: besides effusions in the neo-romantic style, naturalistic poems with misery as their theme, and the ballad-like verses dealing with the Thirty Years War (*Charcoal Sketches after Callot*), they contain chiefly descriptive poems about the streets, houses, churches, and bridges of old Prague, lyrical city views, impressionistic pictures and homage to the Bohemian homeland and its people.

The praises of figures from legend and history are sung, Emperor Rudolf, Jan Hus, wise Rabbi Löw; Czech poets such as the famous dramatist Kajetan Tyl, and also contemporary figures like Julius Zeyer and Jaroslaw Vrchlický are extolled. Czech fragments are placed affectionately in the German verses. Racial tensions which had also become very noticeable in Prague in the 90's and were strong enough to lead to political assassinations are not only ignored here but deliberately denied. The Czech-German symbiosis appears once more here in the light of a euphoric sympathy.

A year later, at Christmas 1896, a third volume of poems appeared in print under the title *Crowned with Dreams*. Here everything is now abandoned again which in *Offering to the Lares* has been gained from the objective outer world: there is a complete inward withdrawal of the lyrical movement. Neo-romantic sentimentality is in full flower. All the paraphernalia of a pre-Raphaelite solemnity are brought into use. Here we see the triumph of a voluptuous soul-lyricism enamored of its own affectation, the narcissistic self-worship of tender, dreamy, and melancholy feelings, and the verse structure has already begun to show occasionally signs of a languishing, voluptuous rhyme-filled "musicality" which later became so popular with *The Book of Hours*.

Similar in key but more varied in thematic invention is the volume *Advent,* which appeared at the end of 1897. Most of the poems in this collection were written in Munich, some during a journey to Venice which the poet undertook in March of that year together with Nathan Sulzberger, a young American with literary pretensions, and a few in Wolfratshausen in the Isar valley. The elements of the naturalistic style have now quite disappeared, although the theme of poverty remains, and there is no hint of the ballad, even sketchbook pictures of towns and landscapes are less numerous. What at this phase Rilke praises about Maeterlinck, the "doctrine of the silent life," that irresistible power of the inner self which is also reminiscent of *Munch,* becomes increasingly the dominant theme of his poetry. The longing of waiting girls or the silent presentiment of expectant mothers kindles his imagination. The future poet of "world-inwardness" is on the point of concentrating his talent, hitherto so uncertain and rambling, upon one single, individual, and authoritative message.

Of these four introductory volumes of poetry only the first, *Life and Songs,* was completely disowned after a very short time by Rilke and even withdrawn from circulation. Throughout his life he conceded a relative justification for the existence of all the others. However, in later years his judgment of his own beginnings was extremely severe. Let us take for example a letter of August 17th, 1924, to the literary historian Hermann Pongs, in which he speaks of his youth with a subtle mixture of shame and gratitude (to his friends and patrons).

"To those overcrowded years when I was busy in every way belongs the period of my earliest and often liveliest productivity, in spite of all the obligations and tasks; my first work was published then—, all those attempts and improvisations which, a short time later, I might have wished I had had the good sense to leave in the drawer of my desk. That they nevertheless escaped, and indeed were thrust out by all the means in my power, is due to the same reason for which today they seem so unsuited to represent the beginnings of my development leading gradually to success. If I was foolish enough to desire to exploit those trifles, it was because of the impatient wish to prove to a reluctant circle my right to such an activity—, a right for which others might like to speak out once these attempts had been displayed. What I hoped for most of all was this: to find in the outside world people who could help me to enter into contact with those currents of thought from which I believed myself to be pretty well cut off in Prague, even if my circumstances had been better than they were. It is the only time in my life that I did not inwardly grapple with work but went out with its feeble beginnings to seek recognition: this above all is probably the reason why, shortly afterwards, after having found my individual nature (about a year before my first journey to Russia) in a provisional center, I disowned with a certain feeling of shame that very early period although its dust still lay thick on my books. In doing so, I was of course condemning my own attitude only and not forgetting the help I had received. In Prague, Alfred Klaar, Friedrich Adler and, among younger supporters, Hugo Salus and the artist Orlik had noticed my work, and August Sauer had already given my earliest attempts an attention which they could not deserve."

If that splendid man Sauer (1855–1926), one of the leading German teachers of that time, could already speak so highly of the poetic activity of the grammar school boy and student, all those should think again who are of the opinion that all Rilke's earliest work, alien as it must seem now that taste has changed, is worthless. But the poet can quote a second name to support this critical self-justification of his youth:

"But the strongest hand which I was privileged to hold was stretched out to me from the north and I must have been really proud of it and did not let it go. I shall never forget that it was Detlev von Liliencron who was one of the first to encourage me to continue the purpose the end of which could not be foreseen —and when occasionally he began his cordial letters with that generous salutation which, when read aloud, ran: 'My excellent René Maria,' it seemed to me (and I endeavored to offer this conviction to my family) that this line was the most reliable indication of my boldest future!"

It is true: Liliencron was the only contemporary master of the

Rilke aged 21. Caricature by Emil Orlik, 1896.

highest class whose example and support inspired and greatly encouraged the young poet when he was in Prague. His influence can be seen most strongly in the *Offering to the Lares*, but it can also be traced in some impressionistic verses of *Crowned with Dreams*.

Liliencron (who had gotten to know Prague during the campaign of 1866 and had received his baptism of fire in Bohemia) spoiled his young admirer with generous letters. Rilke showed his gratitude in every way. When, in the autumn of 1896, it became known in Munich that the Holstein poet was in serious financial difficulties, not only did he write an enthusiastic article about *Poggfred* which had appeared in the *Deutsches Abend-blatt* in January 1897, but he also made it a point of honor to organize from Munich a reading recital in Prague consisting of the works of Liliencron and for the author's benefit. Rilke himself was the reader, and, although the press was somewhat reserved in its opinion, he could not refrain from sending a superlative telegram to Munich: "Liliencron evening great success! materially and ideally! am sending dear Detlev 300 marks

Detlev von Liliencron. Etching by John Philip, 1898.

today and the assurance of many new enthusiastic friends! Long live Liliencron!" And in fact a few months later the author of *Poggfred* and *Adjutantenritte* was himself invited to Prague by the reading circle which Rilke had brought into being; on May 11th, he gave his first reading there and received a warm welcome. About this time Rilke had already begun to move away from Liliencron and to pay homage to other, "more modern" gods. But traces of his gratitude can still be detected even when he moved to Paris. Demetz has, for example, proved that the names which he used in his novel to create atmosphere were largely borrowed from Liliencron's world and works: Malte, Christoph Detlev, and the noble patronymic Brigge itself.

LOU AND RUSSIA

RILKE'S first stay in Munich lasted with some interruptions to the beginning of October 1897. He had some not very close contact with the university, studied a little history of art, especially Italian, but was chiefly concerned with himself, with some new acquaintances and his own poetic activity which was still provisional. Among the writers of his own age who were living in the Bavarian capital there were two especially with whom he became friendly, Wilhelm von Scholz and Jakob Wassermann. He shared with both the pathos of a departure into a new, liberating epoch of artistic expression. "The pictorial splendor of old Gobelins is there," he wrote in a review of Scholz's volume of poems *Hohenklingen* (1897), "and also the tenderness with which the sun gives radiance to their colors . . . the beginnings and the harmonies of a new and mature art." Ardent dedications were exchanged, and Rilke was one of the few guests to be present at Scholz's wedding celebration; he visited

1897.

his friend at the beautiful property of his father, a former Prussian minister of finance, at Lake Constance and—soon afterwards moved away from him. In *Ewald Tragy,* the short story we have already mentioned, he has described with almost autobiographical accuracy his departure from Prague, the flight from the oppressive atmosphere of the Sunday family gathering for luncheon with his aunts Gabriele Kutschera von Woborski and Malwine von Rilke (the widow of Uncle Jaroslaw) and the scarcely less oppressive freedom or rather exposure of his early days in Munich. The distressing grotesqueness of family intercourse (which already foreshadows certain family scenes from *Malte*) has been caught here, although with immature means, just as well as that agonizing, provincial existence led as subtenant by an unknown young son of the Muses who at one and the same time cultivates his loneliness and exploits it in cafés frequented by the literary world. The two friends appear under the name of Wilhelm von Kranz and Thalmann; Scholz, by the way, in a satirical form, which explains at this later date why Rilke's friendship with him had so quickly cooled off.

Jens Peter Jacobsen. Etching by Axel Helsted, 1895.

It was at this time that Rilke learned to read thoroughly and intensively; he ranged widely and endeavored by diligence and discipline to make up for that drawback of a late development which he felt so painfully. As a young man, the writer who had been most significant for him during his reading was Lilien-cron, but now he discovered that author who impressed him as no other did—either earlier or later—and was crucial for his inner self: Jens Peter Jacobsen. What a lasting effect the Dane had on him he has once more stated very clearly in the letter to Pongs in 1924 which has already been quoted:

"But, as for J. P. Jacobsen, even later and for many years, I have gotten from him more than I can describe, so much so that I am unable without deception and invention to assess what he may have meant to me during those earliest years. For a long time after I had moved to Paris he was a mental companion and a spiritual presence; sometimes it seemed to be an unbearable deprivation that he was no longer alive, but it was just this strange compulsive feeling that I had really known him which at an early age produced in me freedom and frankness when thinking of the dead man; an attitude which was subsequently to find the strangest confirmation precisely in Jacobsen's homeland and in Sweden."

What then was this "indescribable" element in the effect which this author had on Rilke as a young man? Was it, as some researchers think, Jacobsen's "ethos of his own death" that fascinated him, or, as others suppose, the special way in which the themes of childhood and girlhood are treated, was it the motif of "letting oneself fall," that strange Nordic atmosphere in general, the cultivation of the "silent life" which he knew of from Maeterlinck and now found transposed into Danish and a subtle narrative style, or were there just certain artistic devices which could be learned from him? The reply must be that it was all this together and that it added up to more than the sum of the details. Whenever some artist was an experience or a model for Rilke, the poet was not beguiled only by single good qualities or single motifs: the great artists who could gain his affection have the same meaning for him as his spiritual homes, they represent the entirety of human things, indeed, of "being" in general in a particular intensive degree of feeling. Just as his own poetic relation to reality can be understood only as an "accomplishment" of the whole through feeling, of the "unity of life and death" (which is to be the final formula), so his admiration for a great artist always means being in complete accord with the entirety of his "nature." That is why, even decades after his intense enthusiasm for Jacobsen, he can confess in a letter to the Zurich literary historian Alfred Schaer (February 16th, 1924): "The name Jacobsen alone signifies quite a definite epoch in my life: he was really the star guiding my decisive years."

Finally, the letter to Pongs explains how these miraculous works came into Rilke's possession: "Actually it was Jakob Wassermann to whom I give the credit for first drawing my attention, almost sternly, to these books (as well as to Turgenev); my lyrical vagueness at that time made him impatient, as he had already learned to value and practice work and elaboration in his life as an artist—, and so, one day in Munich, as a kind of exercise, he put into my hands these works which he had made authoritative for himself a short time previously. That I was unable to find on my own initiative such easily accessible books reminds me of my deplorable helplessness in reading; but for the famous cases of books along the Seine embankment which put within one's reach the works of all ages—, what should I have ever found?"

But a certain experience was far more stimulating in degree than any kind of "influence" or literary contact with the exception of that with Jacobsen: "—but then came the influence of Russia, two years before I traveled there; it was due to a person who was close to me and who summed it up in her own nature, and now, as you correctly realize, the way to my own individual insight was prepared."

This person who was "close to him" and who, born in St. Petersburg, seemed to embody the Russian attitude to life and was later to accompany the poet on his two journeys into the Russian reality was a woman: Lou Andreas-Salomé. Her name stands for a crucial stroke of fate, a decisive landmark in Rilke's biography. It designates not just the first complete love experience of the poet, who was then twenty-one, but also the joy of being understood and led by a like-minded and yet superior soul, and of being able to discern in the beloved the mother figure which he so painfully missed, but above all it designates the great theme of a friendship between equals lasting for decades, an inexhaustibly productive relationship based on confidence, which only the poet's death would bring to an end.

Lou Salomé was born on February 12, 1861; she was the daughter of a Russian general descended from French Huguenots and a German mother. She was thirty-six years of age when she met Rilke. In 1887 she had married Friedrich Carl Andreas (1846–1930), a professor of West-Asiatic languages (in Berlin and later, from 1903, in Göttingen). Earlier she had a friendship with another man of genius, Friedrich Nietzsche, who had asked in vain for her hand in marriage. Later on in life her passion for psychiatric and especially psychoanalytical problems brought her into contact with Sigmund Freud also, and his doctrine became more and more the center of her interests. She became acquainted with Rilke in Munich towards the middle of May 1897, having arrived there from her residence in Schmargendorf near Berlin with the intention of making a fairly long stay. Rilke had very respectfully asked permission to visit the "famous authoress," the writer of a book on Nietzsche and of the story of Ruth which was then very popular, but the earliest of his letters from these weeks were very soon being written in a tone between respect and enamored ardor. Between June 6th and 8th, the tender you (*Sie*) he used was displaced by a passionate thou (*du*):

"I want to see the world through you; for then I shall not be seeing the world but only you, you, you!

"I have never seen you without thinking that I should like to pray to you. I have never heard you without thinking that I should like to believe in you. I have never longed for you without thinking that I should like to suffer for you. I have never desired you without thinking that I should be allowed to kneel before you."

Note the religious language used in this "worship" of the motherly woman. The ardor of erotic homage becomes mystical fire, the words feel for the primeval patterns of mystical rhetoric.

On June 14th Rilke and Lou together with her friend Frieda von Bülow went out to rural Wolfratshausen in the Isar valley and spent the summer there, occasionally in the company of the architect Endell and other friends. When Lou returned home to Berlin on October 1st, Rilke too exchanged the Bavarian for the Prussian capital and took a room for himself in Wilmersdorf for a period which was to last until July 1st of the following year. In Berlin he attended lectures, including those of the philosopher Georg Simmel and the historian Kurt Breysig, and studied the history of art during the Italian Renaissance, but he was to be found more often in museums, exhibitions, and theaters than in the lecture rooms of the university. His meeting with George at the house of Reinhold and Sabine Lepsius belongs to this time (November 14th, 1897) but no closer relationship developed, although, in a letter to the older poet, Rilke begged for the privilege to belong to the reading circle of the Blätter für die Kunst which was chosen by the members, and in spite of an early renewal of the acquaintanceship in Florence in April 1898.

For some time the relationship with Lou was the paramount human contact, indeed this friendship was for three whole years the planet dominating the course of his life. When in April 1898, after first visiting his mother in Arco on Lake Garda, he traveled on to Florence, he gave to a diary which he began to write there the form of an account of his journey intended for the woman he loved. Landscapes, works of art, meditations, aphorisms about everything occupying his mind were supposed in some measure to have been experienced and elaborated under

40

her spell. One has the impression now that there is more precision and discipline in his language, and that his imagination is beginning now to concentrate on some fundamental themes: the artist's world, motherhood, death, history, "God" as he understands the word, and the balance, the "harmonious whole" of life and death. But all this, all this progress, he feels, represents an insufficient effort to catch up spiritually with Lou, to come a little closer to her superiority. *The Tuscan Diary* was

Lou Andreas-Salomé.

continued in May 1898 in Viareggio on the Ligurian coast and completed only at the beginning of July in Zoppot "on the shores of a cooler sea" after he had left Italy and made another journey by way of Prague and Berlin. Towards the end of the manuscript the author turns once again as he had done at the beginning to address Lou directly and to present to her as an offering the new book which he believes to be a "victory."

On July 31st, 1898, Rilke gave up his room in Wilmersdorf in order to settle quite close to Lou and her husband in Schmargendorf at the villa Waldfrieden where he remained till the beginning of October 1900. A few lines from Lou's memoirs give some idea of the setting and the neighborly life together: "Rainer shared fully our humble existence on the edge of the Schmargendorf Wood near Berlin from which a few minutes' walk took us to the wood leading towards Paulsborn past tame deer which sniffed at our coat pockets as we walked barefooted —as my husband had taught us to do."

It was in this year that all the poems of a collection of love lyrics for his friend were written which was to bear the title *In Your Honor* but was never published. To the same year belong all the poems of the volume *In My Honor,* which Rilke sometimes called his first noteworthy work and published in 1899 with the art work done by the Worpswede artist Heinrich Vogeler and bearing for the first time the name Rainer instead of René. *The White Princess* too dates from this time; it is a dramatic scene, deeply tragic in nature, which had been conceived in Viareggio. The theme of love and death is treated with feverish exaltation and over-refined affectation and extravagance. It is about a stately villa with a balcony looking out on to the sea, the sixteenth century, a woman who, in a marriage remaining unconsummated for eleven years, has saved herself for the man who was to come, and the Black Death which ruins everything forever at the critical moment. The new volume of poems is divided into several groups under such characteristic titles as "Songs

42

of Angels," "Maiden Figures," "Songs of Maidens," "Prayers of the Maidens to Mary," or epigraph poems such as "That Is Longing: to Live in the Waves," or "Our Dreams Are Marble Columns." An insatiable languishing and wooing with quite frequently feminine and infantile layers of feeling is coupled with an equally insatiable and now brilliantly developed rhyming skill and is poured out in numerous facile examples. Many of these poems have become very famous and not without good reason. For what they represent is not the trashy flowering of some trivial feelings, but the sentimental early version of an important motif, world-inwardness.

The first journey to Russia, which had been planned for some time and had been mentioned in a letter written in the summer of 1808, was finally undertaken in the spring of 1899. On April 25th the three of them set out from Berlin: Rilke, Lou, and her husband. On April 27th, Maundy Thursday of the orthodox calendar, they were in Moscow and on the evening of the 28th were already being received by the great Leo Tolstoy, then seventy-one. Easter night was celebrated in the Kremlin and was an overpowering event which the poet never forgot throughout his life. "For me there was one Easter," he wrote five years later to Lou from Rome: "It was then in that long, unfamiliar, uncommon, excited night when all the people pressed forward and Ivan Velikij struck me in the darkness, blow on blow. That was my Easter, and I believe it will last me a whole lifetime; that night in Moscow the message that was given to me was strangely grand, it was given me in my blood and in my heart."

Rilke made the acquaintance of the Russian painter Leonid Pasternak and the very famous Elia Repin; from May 4th until June 17th he was in St. Petersburg, living with Lou's relations, and spent three full and exciting weeks among pictures and people before going back to Moscow for three days. The journey home was by way of Danzig and Zoppot and on July 1st he was back in Berlin.

Intense as they were, these first experiences of Russia were too fragmentary and needed to be deepened and widened by theoretical study. Rilke and Lou decided to pursue a systematic course in preparation for a second journey. During a six weeks' stay at Bibersberg near Meiningen, the summer residence of their common friend Frieda von Bülow, they became so involved in their program of study that their hostess could not help feeling neglected. In a letter dated September 20th she complained: "I have seen very little indeed of Lou and Rainer while we were together during these six weeks. After the long journey to Russia which they had undertaken (with Loumann) this spring, they had devoted themselves body and soul to the study of Russian and worked the whole day with phenomenal industry; language, literature, history of art, world history, Russian history, as if they were preparing for some dreadful examination. When we met at mealtimes, they were so tired and exhausted that no *stimulating* conversation ever took place."

The second, longer journey to Russia, which was to take in the South as well, was begun on May 7th, the starting point again being Berlin. This time Rilke was alone with Lou. From May 9th till May 31st they stayed in Moscow and then went to Tula from where they intended to try to obtain a second meeting with Count Tolstoy on his country estate of Yasnaya Polyana. The adventurous mood of those days and the awe in which they stood of the powerful personality of the great Russian author is vividly expressed in a letter from Rilke to Sofia Nikolevna Schill, a writer living in Moscow:

"We drove back as far as Yasnaya, hired a carriage there, and raced with the bells ringing breathlessly to the edge of the hill on which stand the poor huts of Yasnaya crowded into a village, but without any cohesion, like a herd of animals standing sadly on pasture that has been grazed bare. Women and children in groups are only red, sunny flecks in the uniform grey which covers the ground, the roofs, and the walls like a very thick moss

44

Tolstoy in his study.

that has been overgrowing everything for centuries. Then the
road drops, scarcely recognizable, stretching eternally away under
empty spaces, and its grey strip glides gently into a green, well
wooded valley, in which to the left two round little towers sur-
mounted by green cupolas stand at the entrance to the old neglected grounds in which stands secretly the simple house of
Yasnaya Polyana. At this gate we alight and walk quietly like
pilgrims up the quiet wood-lined road until the house stands out,
long and white. A servant takes our cards in. And after a time
we see the figure of the count behind the door in the dark hall of

the house. The eldest son opens the glass door, and we stand inside facing the count, that patriarch, to whom one always comes like a son, even if one has no intention of remaining in his fatherly power. He seems to have become smaller, whiter, more bent, and, as if independent of the aged body, the un-shadowed, clear eye awaits the strangers and scrutinizes them deliberately and blesses them involuntarily with some unutterable blessing . . ."

Later they take a walk together through the park: "we walk slowly down the long, overgrown paths, deep in conversation to which the count lends warmth and animation as he did before. He speaks Russian and, when the wind does not drown the words, I can understand every syllable. He has thrust his left hand under his woollen jacket into his belt, his right hand rests on the top of his stick without leaning heavily on it, and he stoops from time to time, with a movement as if he were going to gather a flower with the fragrance enveloping it, but he picks some herb and drinks the aroma out of the hollow of his hand, and, without interrupting the conversation, he drops the empty flower indifferently into the rich superfluity of the wild spring, which has not suffered any impoverishment.—The conversation covers many things. But all the words do not pass by in front of them, keeping to the externals, they penetrate through in darkness behind the things. And the profound value of each word is not its color in the light, but the feeling that it comes from the darkness and the mystery out of which we all live. And whenever, in the sound of the conversation, the non-mutual became apparent, a glimpse was afforded of bright backgrounds of deep unity . . . Sometimes the count's figure grew in the wind; the great beard blew, but the grave face marked by loneliness remained calm, as if untouched by the storm . . ."

From Tula they went to holy Kiev where they stayed fourteen days. Rilke received lasting impressions from art and history; the piety of the people overpowered him to such a degree that

Rilke, Lou Andreas-Salomé, and the Russian peasant poet Spiridon Drozhin.

he himself joined in a religious procession with a candle in his hand. Then they went by boat on the Dnieper to Kremenchug, and from there by way of Poltava and Kharkov to Voronezh, then in an easterly direction to Saratov on the Volga. From June 25th until the morning of July 2nd they traveled by boat upstream to Yaroslavl, passing Simbirsk (Ulyanovsk), Kazan, and Nizhni Novgorod. The couple spent three unforgettable days among the peasants of a village near Yaroslavl and were back in Moscow on July 6th where they remained until the 18th. A final outstanding event in the journey was the visit they paid to the peasant poet Spiridon Drozhin (1848–1930), whose lyrics

47

Rilke had already translated and published, in Nisovka on the Upper Volga and to his landlord, Count Nikolai Tolstoy. "During these days," Rilke wrote to Sofia Schill, "we are getting close to the heart of Russia, for whose beats we have long been listening, with the feeling that they will give us the right frequency for our own lives." At the end of July they were back in St. Petersburg where they had to separate for three weeks. Lou went to visit relatives in Finland, Rilke remained in the city, working in libraries and meeting artists and intellectuals. Nevertheless, he found this brief separation from his beloved very difficult to bear and asked her to return sooner than she had intended. On August 22nd they took the train for Berlin together.

During these years Rilke passionately absorbed everything that was Russian, great literature and mediocre painting, translated a good deal, Chekhov, some of Dostoevsky, and later Lermontov too. He himself wrote a series of poems in Russian and in 1902 tried to render into German the old epic *Song of Igor's March*. "That Russia is my homeland," he wrote in a letter to Lou on August 15th, 1903, "is one of those great and mysterious certainties which form the basis of my life." It is not the only country which he wanted to claim as his homeland; in a letter (March 17th, 1926) to a "young friend, a girl," he says there are: ". . . many countries in which, owing to the constant patience and forbearance of my fate, I have been privileged not just to stay as a traveler but really to live, in the liveliest contact with the present and the past of these countries." But the same letter, written a few months before his death, also confesses: "Russia (as you know from books such as *The Book of Hours*) was, in a certain sense, the basis on which I felt and received, just as, from the year 1902 Paris—the incomparable—became the basis on which I sought to give my work shape."

Rilke could never feel that Prague, Munich, or Berlin was both city and home. By home he meant the entire human scene in a peculiarly "intimate" and "deep" openheartedness. Home is the whole of existence as it is revealed, in a form canonized by feeling. The moods of being can vary, it may be Paris, Toledo, Sweden, or Italy. With Russia it is something shapeless and elemental, a powerful, brotherly constellation of "God," "people," and "nature." It is the "creation" character of existence as the young poet describes it in a note written in St. Petersburg on July 31st, 1900: "to be for days and nights, for many days and many nights on the Volga, this peacefully rolling sea. A broad, broad stream, tall, tall forest on one bank, on the other side deep heathland, in which even great cities only look like huts and tents.—One has to relearn all dimensions. One has this experience: land is big, water is something big, and above all the sky is big. What I saw until now was only an image of land and river and world. But here everything is itself.—I feel as if I had witnessed creation; few words for all being, things in the proportion of God the Father . . ."

Rilke never denied this newly won certainty. Even under the dominating influence of his second and seemingly so contrasting spiritual home, Paris, it remained sacred to him. At a time when Rodin and antiquity were already standing in the foreground of his consciousness, and the essence of being, the final state of world-being for him, was no longer "God" but "thing," he did not abandon his very personal Russia myth but tried to find what it had in common with the Paris myth. So we find him writing to Lou in the letter of August 15th which has already been mentioned:

"Just as great are Gothic things too which, although they are much nearer in time, are just as remote, just as nameless, just as independent in their loneliness, without origin like things in nature. They and what came from Rodin's hands led us back to the most remote art—things, done by people before the Greeks, in whose essence lies his sculptural recklessness, a thingness which is as heavy as lead, mountain-like and hard. Affinities were revealed which nobody as yet has felt, associations were formed and currents established which go through the ages, and the history of infinite generations of things could be surmised under the history of mankind, like a structure of slower and quieter developments which happen more deeply, more inwardly, and more unswervingly. Into this history, Lou, Russian man will perhaps one day fit, creatively like Rodin, as one who, becoming and enduring, descends from things and is related to them, blood-related. That patient waiting in the Russian character (which the German with his self-important preoccupation with the unimportant calls laziness) would thus receive a new and certain elucidation: perhaps the Russian has been made to let the history of mankind go by him so that later he can join in the harmony of things with his singing heart. He has only to endure, to hold out, and, like the violinist to whom no signal has yet been given, to sit in the orchestra carefully holding his instrument, so that nothing may happen to it . . ."

The Russia motif accompanied the poet right up to those great harvest days in February 1922 when the *Duino Elegies* were completed and the whole corpus of the *Sonnets to Orpheus* was conceived: an event which is not linked with its biographical date. What had once already born such poetic fruit at that early stage of development seen in *The Book of Hours* is now represented afresh in the clear and bold language of mastery and is transformed into the Orphic associations of "singing" and "hearing":

> But what shall I offer you, Master, say,
> you who taught all creatures to hear?
> The remembered evening of one spring day,
> in Russia; a horse drawing near . . .
>
> White, coming up from the village alone,
> on one fetlock a tethering-block,
> to spend the night alone, on his own:
> how gaily he tossed the shock

of his mane in time to his mounting mood
on that rudely encumbered race!
How they leapt, the springs of that equine blood!

He had followed the call of space.
He sang and he listened—your circle swept
unbrokenly through him.
      His image: accept.

These are the words of the twentieth sonnet in the first part
of the Orphic cycle. In a joyful and excited letter to Lou on
February 11th, 1922, announcing the completion of the *Elegies,*
Rilke also tells her how this poem came into being:

". . . and imagine, something else, in a different connection
just before [in the *Sonnets to Orpheus,* twenty-five sonnets written suddenly, in a rush, as a monument for Wera Knoop] I
wrote, *made* the Horse, do you remember, the free, happy, white
horse dragging a picket, which galloped towards us one evening
in a meadow by the Volga—:
                    how
I made him, as an *ex voto* for Orpheus!—What is time? When
is the present? Across so many years, with all his happiness, he
rushed into my wide-open feelings."

The lifelong permanence of those Russian experiences was
matched by the almost unbroken continuity of his friendship
with his traveling companion of that time. Only once, at the
beginning of 1901, when Rilke was about to be completely
caught up in his new circle of friends in Worpswede, was there
a sort of crisis with Lou, and a gap of almost two and a half
years intervened in the correspondence. A "final salutation" from
his friend who had ceased to be his beloved was couched in confused, if not embarrassing, speculations about the dangers of his
excessively sensitive nature, which she believed was threatened
by a psychical disturbance, and it concluded with a farewell
blessing for the future:

". . . and I now know very clearly and send you these words: follow the same road towards your dark God! He can do what I am no longer able to do for you . . ." (February 21, 1901).

They broke away from one another with the "vow" not to write again "except in the hour of the greatest distress." But in the early days in Paris the relationship had already been fully re-established, and there were to be moments later when nobody in the whole world would seem to be so close to the poet as Lou and when she would be the only person empowered by Rilke in his solitude to take over the role of the *vox humana:* "I often tell myself that I only communicate with mankind through you, in you it is turned towards me, is aware of me, breathes on me: everywhere else I somehow find its back turned towards me and cannot make myself known to it."

WORPSWEDE AND WESTERWEDE

BETWEEN the second stay in Russia and his first arrival in Paris on August 28th, 1902, there intervened the two years which Rilke spent chiefly in the circle of the artists' colony in Worpswede which was then flourishing: living among new friends and women and finally even founding his own household, as the husband of a young artist and father of her only child. It was a short-lived attempt to overcome the absence of commitment during a lifelong pilgrimage, to acquire among scenery he loved not only inner but also bourgeois rights of domicile, and to some extent to correct the "non-commitment" of his soul which he often felt so painfully by consenting to the fate which marriage would mean. Worpswede, a small, unpretentious market town situated between Bremen and Hamburg, had, about the year 1900, become the outpost and embodiment of a progressive artistic activity. A new kind of landscape painting which eschewed the academic had discovered the plain and its immense sky, the marsh and heath, and the characteristic stature and lines of the heavy-limbed and introspective race of men which could only thrive in those parts. A remarkable mixture of nature-loving solidity and the typical *fin de siècle* taste for the languishing refinement and effeminacy of the inner life was struggling for expression and laid claim to be a revolutionary breakthrough to "reality." There was about this art something of the walking in bare feet of civilized human beings who were intoxicated with their feelings and full of thoughts impossible to express: Rilke and Lou had practiced this in Schmargendorf and in the fields on the banks of the Volga, and it was precisely because of his journeys to Russia that the poet knew that he was quite ready for the artists' village in the North German plain. How very congenial to the artist's mood the experience of nature was which received expression there, as well as the atmosphere which was cultivated in the colony, he recorded soon afterwards in a little book in the spirit of a friendly confession: it was a collection of lyrical essays which he wrote about the artists Otto Modersohn, Fritz Mackensen, Fritz Overbeck, Hans am Ende, and Heinrich Vogeler and published in 1903 under the title *Worpswede.*

The first of the young painters with whom Rilke came into contact was Heinrich Vogeler, who had been living in Worpswede since 1894. They had already gotten to know one another in Florence early in 1898, and for the first time during the Christmas of the same year the poet was Vogeler's guest in his beautiful house Barkenhoff. They were infatuated with one another and made joint plans of which only a few were put into execution in the course of time, but, even many years later, there was ample evidence of the former cordiality of their relations in the dedication which was placed at the front of *The Life of Mary,* written in Duino as late as 1912: "to Heinrich Vogeler in gratitude for old and new inspiration to write these poems."

In the summer of 1900 Vogeler repeated his invitation to the poet, and the very next day after his return from St. Petersburg Rilke went to Worpswede. This time he stayed for rather more than a month and only returned to Berlin on October 5th.

In his *Worpswede* and in his *Schmargendorf Diary*—the former covers the days to September 26th, the latter the time from September 27th to the end of the year, Rilke has described in detail these weeks which were passed in a festive atmosphere and were full of experiences, memorable occasions, and an affectionate and soul-stirring social life. Never before or afterwards did the bliss of being young in the company of like-minded young people take such a deep and absolute hold of him as in the late summer of the year 1900. Never again was he overpowered by the *embarras de richesses* of a life that opened out in all directions and grew more intense with every moment. It is like a crowded fairy tale; time is an unbroken chain of high pitched, even intoxicating days. Through his head there must have been running questions such as: "Where shall I start? Where is the first thread in this dark-colored fabric of events and memories?" The house concerts in the white music room, the reading recitals in which the stranger could give his own poems to a highly appreciative audience, the spontaneous visits to galleries and exhibitions, the nights spent in revelry, madly rushing from one studio to another, and, at the break of day, improvised journeys across country in carriages with the coachman perched high on top, the never-ending conversations, in which they showed a deep understanding of one another as they exchanged early experiences concerning the mysteries of life and death, and finally—at the end of September—a journey together to Hamburg to the premier of a new play by Carl Hauptmann, a friend of the Worpswede colony—not forgetting the great, inexhaustible, and daily-renewed adventure of the landscape: it was all taken as an act of "fate" and seemed to be happening under the most auspicious planets. Two young women were vitally concerned, a fair-complexioned artist and her friend, a tall, dark-haired person who was working on sculptures in her studio: Paula Becker, later to be the wife of Modersohn, and Clara Westhoff, the daughter of a Bremen merchant. Both had already been in Paris, and Clara had studied under Rodin. They were usually together as sisters—"Dr. Hauptmann came down the hill with two sisters, one fair and the other dark," that is how they are introduced—, and from the outset there could be no doubt that it was their company which irresistibly attracted the author of these diaries and became every moment more precious. In an entry on September 10th he recorded:

"The girls, dressed all in white, came down the hill from the heath. The fair-complexioned artist first of all, smiling from under a big Florentine hat. I was up at the studio window, passing a heavy table for paints through to Frau Freitag. The fair artist entitled this scene 'Struggle with the Table,' then I greeted them all . . . Just as we were standing in the dark hall making one another's acquaintance, Clara Westhoff came. She was wearing a dress of white cambric without any bodice, in the Empire style. It was lightly fastened high under the bosom and had long, smooth folds. Round her lovely dark face blew black, light, hanging curls, which she wears loose down both cheeks as the style of her dress demands. —The whole house flattered her, everybody became more attentive, seeming to adapt themselves to her, and when, upstairs, she was leaning on my leather arm-chair listening to the music, she was our acknowledged mistress. That evening I saw her in many beautiful attitudes. When she is listening, the occasionally too emphatic features are concentrated on something unknown . . ."

And later, after the evening seemed to have degenerated into some noisy skylarking: ". . . but the end was beautiful all the same, and that was due to the girls in white. I opened the door of my room where in the darkness it was blue and cool as in a grotto. I pushed open my window, and then they came in to share the wonder and leaned in their bright dresses out into the moonlit night which sent cold air on to their cheeks that were hot from laughing . . . Half aware, as artists, half unconscious, as girls. Then the atmosphere takes hold of them, the whole effect of this misty night with the moon, which is almost full, above the three poplars, this atmosphere of dull, beaten silver makes them defenseless and they are just girls again, full of darkness and longing . . . Then the artist in them regains her power and looks and looks, and when she has looked hard enough, they are back on the threshold of their own being and wonder and slip back into their girlhood . . ."

The breathless excitement of these weeks, every day of which seemed to subside again into moments of intimate happiness or of melting sadness, was nevertheless basically moving towards something final, decisive. In the air there was a general feeling of nuptial expectation: at the end of the year six of the friends

Paula Becker and Clara Westhoff.

would be married. Not only would Heinrich Vogeler have taken beautiful Martha Schröder, who according to Rilke was a figure out of *Munch,* surrounded by mystery and timid reserve, and made her the mistress of Barkenhoff, but for the poet also, for Modersohn and the two "sisters," the dice would have been cast.

There is much to suggest that Rilke at that time really felt affection amounting to a kind of passion for the "fair artist" and not for Clara Westhoff, later to become his wife. If this impression is not mistaken, his sudden and almost discourteous departure on October 5th would be connected with the engagement of Paula Becker to Modersohn about which he heard at that time. It is certainly true that his visits to what he calls Paula's "lily studio" are described with a loving concern that seems to go somewhat beyond that state of constant emotion, and the conversations that were held there touched upon the central themes of Rilke's thinking and writing and bear witness to the frankness of their mutual trust:

"Then I went to the lily studio. Tea was waiting. Together we shared conversation and silence, and it was good and rich. Evening came marvelously; we spoke about: Tolstoy, death, Georges Rodenbach, Hauptmann's *Friedensfest,* life and beauty in all experience, the ability and the will to die, eternity and why we feel related to the eternal. About so many things passing beyond the hour and ourselves. Everything became mysterious. The clock struck a very late hour and its chime was loud as it passed round and through our conversation. —Her hair was of Florentine gold. In her voice there were folds like silk. I had never seen her so slim in her maidenliness. A great shadow passed through the room . . . first over me, the speaker, over my desultory words, then over her bright figure and over all the gleaming objects. We looked at the windows facing the west. But nobody had passed close by."

And yet, a few lines further on, we are back again with the double figure of the two friends, and his homage is being addressed to them both, it is the "miracle," the Rilke myth of girl-hood in general.

Neither can draw from him a quite unmistakable confession of love. The truth is that both of them provide the same stimulus for his feelings which are seeking enjoyment and for that balancing act between two affections which mutually neutralize one another: "and I always strive softly to rock their souls with my changing words but no pan moves and they play in the two shores of equilibrium."

This strange indecision in a situation which, according to bourgeois notions, would call for a very responsible decision, gives evidence of the inner constitution of a man who wants to reveal his feelings even when he is in love and has to transfer into "art" all the experiences life has to offer him. To be an artist means to neutralize "life," to create distance while the surrender is taking place, and the dilemma of artistic existence consists of that unwillingness to submit to fate which constitutes his fate; this is what Rilke means by the words in the ninth elegy: "shunning destiny, longing for destiny." And it is possible therefore that the writer of this most impassioned praise of women in modern poetry could never during his lifetime succumb to an erotic passion, never belong to any woman. He found the formula in his "Requiem" for Paula Becker (1908):

> "for somewhere is old hostility
> between life and one's great work . . ."

but here already in Worpswede where he praises in both friends the presence and contrast of girlish "longing" and artistic "gazing," he has in mind the same conflict. All the accounts he gives of experiences in these diaries are prose exercises based on the material of the senses and the feelings, they are attempts to educate himself to ever greater accuracy and justice of portrayal: "We walked together through the heath, it was evening and windy. And walking in Worpswede is always like this; for a time one goes on, in conversation, which the wind quickly destroys, —then somebody stops and after a while somebody else. So much is happening. Under the immense skies the darkening, colored fields lie flat, there are distant shapes of hills, tall, swaying heather, and nearby stubble fields and buckwheat which has just been mown; with the red of its stems and the yellow of its leaves it is like an exquisite silken material. And how it all lies there, close and so real that one cannot miss it or forget it. Every moment something is caught in the sunny air, a tree, a house, a mill, turning quite slowly, a man with black shoulders, a large cow or a sharply angular, jagged goat, standing out against the sky."

In this sense people too can become the subject of studies with an objective tendency: the intensity of feeling which at its origin was directed at some living girl is at the same time something "productive" and in process of being understood as due to the *artistic* gift and of being transformed into the poet's mind, which remains at a distance.

After returning from Hamburg Rilke wrote in his diary on September 27th: "A lovely, quiet, starry night, homecoming was festive and good. And so I decided to remain in Worpswede. I have begun to feel now how the solitude increases every day, how this land devoid of colors and shadow, grows bigger and bigger, wider and wider, providing an ever larger background for trees shaken by the storm. I want to remain in this storm and feel all the thrill of this deeply moving experience. I want autumn. I want to cover myself with winter and do not want to betray myself with any color. I want to lie under the snow for the sake of a spring to come, so that what is growing inside me will not come up from the furrows too soon."

A few days later he was back in Berlin, talking of an indispensable third journey to Russia and the preparations he must make there, and he wrote to Paula Becker: "For me Russia has indeed become what your countryside means to you: home and

59

sky . . ." He wrote in the same strain to Clara Westhoff: "To me your homeland was from the first moment more than just a kind foreign country. It was truly homeland, *the first homeland in which I saw people living* (elsewhere they all live in foreign countries and the homelands are empty . . .)."

And yet he finds it necessary to put in a caution again. "You will understand," he writes to the fair artist, "that it is a breach of faith to behave as if I have found somewhere else a completely satisfying hearth and home. I can still not have any cottage, I can still not have any abode. To wander and wait is my lot."

So Rilke remained for the time being in Schmargendorf where in the meantime—it was in the middle of October—he had exchanged the villa Waldfrieden for a room in Misdroy Strasse. For a time when she was in Berlin at the beginning of 1901, Paula Becker visited him there every Sunday. And the dark-complexioned sister came to Berlin also; the Worpswede constellation seemed to be restored, whether in the shape of a tormented conflict or not. After Paula had left, Rilke and Clara resolved to get married: an event which, for Rilke's part, did not interrupt the continuity of his spiritual life and about which no fuss was made in the very full documentation we possess about his life. In the middle of March, after previously visiting his mother at Lake Garda, he was in Bremen and the marriage took place on April 28th. The couple furnished rooms for themselves in a farmhouse in Westerwede, not far from Worpswede, and they hoped that these would satisfy their artistic requirements. They had very definite and sober views about what marriage meant: "As for the rest, I am of the opinion that 'marriage' as such does not deserve as much emphasis as it has gained from conventional development as an institution. Nobody would think of demanding from a single person that he should be 'happy,' —but if he marries, there is great astonishment if he isn't!"

That is what he wrote to Emanuel Bodman on August 17th,

Rilke and Clara in Westerwede.

1901. It will be understood that Rilke had a marriage between artists especially in mind when he wrote: "I feel that in marriage what matters is not quickly to create a common way of life by toppling and demolishing all barriers, rather is a good marriage one in which each partner sets the other to watch over his solitude, thereby showing him the greatest confidence he has to bestow. It is impossible for two people to be *united* and where this does seem to have happened, it is a restriction, a mutual agreement which deprives one or both of the fullest freedom and development."

On December 12th, 1901, the young couple had a daughter, Ruth. "She has dark hair," they wrote to Franziska Reventlow on December 18th, "quite dark blue eyes, a grave forehead, and quite exquisite hands." But by the autumn of 1902 the child had to be taken to Oberneuland near Bremen to be looked after by the grandparents: the attempt to acquire a permanent home and maintain a family by his own resources had failed.

For one year and one summer Rilke honestly strove to build up something resembling a bourgeois existence and to maintain himself and his dependents by his pen. He supplied abundant copy to journals and newspapers, especially the *Bremer Tageblatt:* book reviews, theater criticism, and short essays dealing with contemporary fine arts. He makes it quite clear in a letter to Otto Modersohn dated June 25th, 1902, what he himself thought about this occupation: "When I write for the *Bremer Tageblatt,* I always write into my beard, keeping my left hand over my mouth, then it sounds more journalistic."

His father's allowance had ceased, there could no longer be any thought of continuing his studies, and material cares were not only putting his marriage in jeopardy but were also threatening the spiritual source of his own productive work. True, he did receive some outside assistance. For example, the respected founder and first director of the Bremer Kunsthalle, Gustav Pauli (1866–1938), secured for him the commission to write about Worpswede for Velhagen and Klasing, and he himself also gave him the opportunity to write a short festival scene for the opening of his museum (1902). But what he needed to be able to maintain three people indefinitely: "work in some editorial office or with a publishing firm, in an art gallery or collection, some theater reviewing or such like," was not forthcoming. Nor could Clara Rilke's plan to work with a number of pupils in Bremen be realized. So there seemed to be no other choice than to give up the attempt to settle down in Westerwede and to resume the old life of travel in order to turn to account the advantages of being strictly alone, of unexpected opportunities, of hospitality with different hosts.

By the early summer of 1902 the poet, in spite of a complete lack of means, could be seen enjoying that luxurious independence such as could only be afforded on the country estates of the late feudal era and was to be his again and again by a characteristically favorable dispensation of fate. Prince Emil von Schönaich-Carolath (1852–1908), a poetically gifted aristocrat, with whom he had remained in touch since the Wegwarten period, had invited him to stay at his seat in Holstein. There he read the proofs of *The Book of Images,* savored after such a long time the solitude, revelled in the beauties of the large, luxuriant, and "not too well-kept" park and felt completely in his element. He was surrounded by all sorts of historical reminders, the Danish family way of life was in the air, and there were the first vague outlines of a new poetic work which was only gradually to take shape in Paris.

From Haseldorf on June 28th he sent his first letter in what was still clumsy French to the great man destined to be the last master and guiding star of his youth, Auguste Rodin. He asked Rodin for his help in an enterprise which was to go far beyond the immediate occasion and open up quite new horizons of seeing, feeling, and creating.

Rilke went to Paris to discharge a quite specific commission and in this way to solve the problem of existence chiefly for himself, but at the same time to come to grips with an artistic and human experience which had recently assumed ever increasing importance and which he wished to study thoroughly and master with all his strength. Clara Rilke also went to Paris in the autumn of 1902 in order to continue her own studies; she too subsequently travelled and spent many years, usually separated from her husband, in European centers of artistic life, and it was only in 1918 that she finally returned to her native country. For more than thirty-five years she had her own house there in Fischerhude near Bremen and only died in 1954 at the age of 76.

The poetic output of the years 1899 to 1902 was again very large, but it was published only in part at that time. Three volumes of narrative prose were printed: *Two Prague Tales* (1899; later renamed *Tales of God*), *The Last of Their Line* (1902), God and Other Stories (1900). Also to appear were: the first edition of the collection of poetry *The Book of Images,* which he had written during the years 1898–1901 and published in 1902, and a play in two acts, *Daily Life* (1902). This last attempt at drama by the poet, written during Easter in 1900, had been performed in December 1901 on a Berlin stage and had given rise to nothing but comic effects as Rilke himself gloomily confessed in a letter to Ellen Key in 1902. Not printed at that time were the two first parts of *The Book of Hours: The Book of the Monastic Life,* written in Schmargendorf in 1899, and *The Book of Pilgrimage,* written in Westerwede in September 1901. Together with the third part of *The Book of Hours* written in Viareggio, they appeared as a whole only at Christmas 1905. To remain equally unknown for the time being was that work by Rilke which during all these decades has had the greatest success and which has carried away several generations of adolescents to storms of enthusiasm and orgies of emotion: *The Lay of the Love and Death of Cornet Christopher Rilke.* The first version of this short work of 14 pages, written in a very lyrical prose that continually broke out into rhyming and extremely rhythmical sequences, had already been written down in the autumn of 1899. The *Cornet,* so the poet wrote, looking back in

Page from the manuscript of the *Cornet* (first version, 1899).

a letter to H. Pongs in 1924: "was the unexpected present of a single night in autumn and was written without a break by the light of two candles flickering in the wind; it was the result of clouds passing across the moon, after the subject had been suggested to me some weeks beforehand by a preliminary study of certain family papers which I had inherited."

This first version of the *Cornet* even failed to find a publisher in those days. A revised version of August 1904 was printed in a Prague journal and it did not appear in book form until the end of 1906. It had no more than a modest success and scarcely 50 copies could be disposed of. Only when the text was taken up again in 1912 did it begin to meet with success, and fifty years later, over a million copies had been sold.

The lyrics of these years reveal in hundreds of attempts, some forward-, others backward-looking, that the poet was in a transitional phase, that his talent had not quite been able to detach itself from the old, well-rehearsed but for that reason really overplayed melodies in the style of *Advent* and *In My Honor,* although he was already looking for new forms and motifs. In *The Book of Images* there are many poems with that sickly, mawkish tone which has now become a cliché and of which "Dawn" is an example, that polypus-like proliferation of end-rhymes, inner-rhymes, alliteration, and all kinds of cheap assonance, that frivolous indulgence in an outworn facility of alternating meter.

Other details are already pointing forward to the greater stress on things, the ethos of work and to the pathos of objectification in *New Poems.* An attitude of looking from a distance begins to assert itself and to grow stronger and stronger: the feeling self wishes to be suspended, to become concrete, to conquer the outside world—"things" and "images"—but remaining ever aware that all outside things are related to it.

To make "images" now means to produce in lyrical form prototype figures, historical and legendary persons and situations, concise résumés of human destinies, and to satisfy with romantic fables his own insatiable feelings which are ever craving for the inexpressible. The result of this is a new variety of ballad style: "Charles the Twelfth" is a prime example. And Rilke's poems based on subjects from Christian doctrine and the passion and salvation of Christ—such as "The Day of Judgment" —follow this line: they are not to be understood as evidence of belief or exercises in piety but as ballads of the soul and sensory expressions of the feelings speculating on some particular text from the scriptures. Strictly speaking, they are parodies of the gospel stories.

But the main lyrical work belonging to these years is *The Book of Hours,* because it embraces under one great cyclic idea all the motifs and lines of thought which are found individually elsewhere. As was to happen later in *Duino Elegies* and the *Sonnets to Orpheus,* there is in this first important cyclic work by Rilke a complete lyrical system, a poetic life-doctrine at an early stage. The word "life" was of course dear to the sentimental souls at the turn of the century: it kept an echo of Nietzschean exultation and Nietzschean suffering, but both Hofmannsthal and Andrian, Wedekind and Dehmel have by their outlook and their works made contributions which have loaded this word with its present fullness of meaning. "When you then spoke about something very dear—or about life": these were the words Rilke used to remind the fair artist of the conversations they had had in Worpswede. At an early stage he was very well aware of what the concept "life" meant to him, and this did not change in the course of his development, in spite of all his artistic improvement.

Life as what is "nameless," the pure unutterable perceptibility of the world with a thousand faces, seeks urgently for some all-embracing expression and the word which offers itself as salvation to the poet of *The Book of Hours* and which has to represent the mysterious unity of the many is no less than the name of God:

> and who then lives it? Do you, dear God,—yes, Life?

How can one characterize the idea of God as found in *The Book of Hours* and in Rilke's work in general? It rests upon notions which are essentially gnostic and is not far removed either from attitudes of thought which are to be found in certain mystical literatures: God is growing, his existence is based in the existence of the feelings and the speculation of a few human hearts. Even in the *Tuscan Diary* (April 1898) there is to be found a passage like this: "God is the most ancient work of art.

67

It is very badly preserved and later many parts have been more or less restored. But, of course, a cultured man must be able to talk about him and he must have seen the remains."

Later, in Worpswede, the poet gave an account of a conversation he had with Paula Becker, who refused to revere under the name of "God" anything other than nature, "she who brings, who has life and bestows it."

"But I spoke softly about him. That his shortcomings, his injustice, and all the inadequacies of his power were due to his development. That he was not yet completed. Moreover, when should he have finished growing? Man needed him so urgently that straight from the beginning he felt and saw him as existing. Man needed him complete, and he said: God is. Now he has to make good his growth. And we are here to give this help. With us and with our joy he grows, and our sadness imprints the shadows on his countenance . . ."

The aversion Rilke felt for the figure of Christ and which was later to assume such gross forms was expressed even in this early work: "For young people (I said this somewhere else) Christ is a great danger; he is too close and hides God. They become used to seeking the divine with human measuring rods. They are spoiled by this human standard and later they freeze to death in the bitter mountain air of eternity. They wander about between Christ, the figures of Mary and the saints: they lose their way among figures and forms . . . They grow resigned, but they should not be resigned if they want to have God."

His own ripening which developed his first full poetic power (I feel: I can) is interpreted as a ripening of God; God is created as a work of art by the force of the feelings and the imagination of many fervent generations:

> We're workmen: all the myriads of us, whether
> craftsman or prentice, huge Nave, building *you*.
> And sometimes comes a keen-faced traveler hither,

streaks like a flash through all our hearts together,
and quivering shows us knacks adroit and new.

It is certainly not wrong to assert that experience of the Russian people's piety had inspired the poet to plan and complete this work. The gold-glittering darkness of icons dominates the atmosphere, Russian stage props are fairly numerous, and God is occasionally described as Lyeskov Starez or a bearded peasant. Yet it would not show a real understanding of the work to pretend to find a genuine religious passion in the author or to dismiss him as a seeker after God. The path that Rilke followed was quite different from the one suggested by this expression and led to his own, independent, very personal myth of "existence," which cannot be interpreted in a religious or a "theological" sense. Even in *The Book of Hours* "things" are extolled as coming from the depths of an inexhaustibly productive existence, with which the productive force of the poet shares solidarity and knows it is identical. (This force is later to be called "nature" or "earth.") Rilke's passion is fundamentally poetical, a passion which must find names, and it is in an abundance of names that he here drowns, as it were, the transcendental reality of God.

The first two books written in prose during this period should be regarded as stragglers from his prentice years; they still follow the pattern of a more or less traditional style of short story with which Rilke's talent cannot do much, or at any rate can do nothing extraordinary. Only the *Tales of God* are related by their subject to *The Book of Hours* but do not reach that standard. In the mannered, childlike tone of the legend, which occasionally lapses into whimsy, the message is preached here that God "is in all things," e.g., in the stone from which Michelangelo carved his figures, or in the thimble which little Resi has taken away from her mother. Finally, as regards the *Cornet*, it just cannot be placed in these surroundings. This most popular creation of Rilke's fantasy stands quite on its own; it is a unique success with a heartfelt and sensuous magic power: "The tunic, the bandolier, and the cloak of von Langenau hang over a chair in the outer room. On the floor lie his gloves. Slender and black his flag stands erect, leaning against the cross of the window. Outside a storm gallops across the sky, tearing fragments of black and of white out of the night. Like a long lightning flash the moonlight passes. And the resting flag has restive shadows. It is dreaming."

It is the story of an eighteen-year-old youth who in a single night experiences love and death, sighed and stormed out in lyrical abbreviations, a feat of bravura, which to some extent has achieved its success outside Rilke's development from a lesser to a higher art: "Racing with passages ablaze through doors that encircle him glowing, over stairs that sear him, he breaks from the raging castle. And like a white unconscious maid the flag in his arms is laid. And then the flag is seen to revive, majestic as never before, and alive. Now all can see it far in front; and, seeing the fair youth without helmet, they know the flag as their own . . . And then it begins to glow, unfurls, and grows immense and red . . . There in the midst of the foe their flag is aflame. And they rally to it."

After its huge success, Rilke later expressed some indignation with this "Cornet" who shouted "like a sergeant-major," and yet, even today the absolutely pure mood of the work, this hot, naked, sobbing, and revelling youthful feeling is so irresistible that its popularity is not surprising.

After its huge success, Rilke later expressed some indignation with this "Cornet" who shouted "like a sergeant-major," and yet, even today the absolutely pure mood of the work, this hot, naked, sobbing, and revelling youthful feeling is so irresistible that its popularity is not surprising.

Echoes of this intoxicated, crowded time which was so full of decisions affecting people and his art, and which culminated in these September days in Worpswede, reached far into the years spent in Paris. Paula Becker, who had married Otto Modersohn at Whitsuntide 1901, a few weeks after Rilke's wedding, was frequently in Paris where she met the poet. Rilke understood very late what an extraordinary artist she was. Even at the beginning of 1903 he was recommending her in a letter to Rodin as "la femme d'un peintre allemand très distingué," and only three years later, in an account of a Christmas visit to Worpswede (to Karl von der Heydt) does he show himself moved by her work: "What was most remarkable was to find Modersohn's wife at a quite distinctive stage of her development, painting heedlessly and frankly things which were very typical of Worpswede and which however nobody had yet been able to see and paint. And, while taking this quite personal line, in strange contact with van Gogh and his art."

In May 1906 he sat as a model for his friend: the portrait which then resulted, although unfinished, is a masterpiece of expressionist painting and the only painting of the poet which is equal to its subject. It foreshadows the poet Rilke as he had not yet become and as he would be only twenty years later, the poet of the *Elegies* and the *Sonnets*. It shows the extraordinary mouth of this man just as Rudolf Kassner once described it: "Rilke's face ended at the mouth, opened in the mouth and became here an opening. After or below such a mouth there can be no chin of any importance. About this great mouth which existed for the words to open into something great, greater, universal, there is something unhealthy, dead. How that agrees with his doctrine that each man must die his own death, bring forth his own death!"

Rilke, who on other occasions could be very outspoken about his portraits, never mentioned Paula Becker's work. What this radical artist was aiming at in her lonely struggle, what modern painting under the triple star van Gogh-Gauguin-Cézanne could be, perhaps *had* to be, came to him like a revelation only in the autumn of 1907 when he stood in front of the great exhibition in

Rilke. Unfinished portrait by Paula Modersohn-Becker.

memory of Cézanne at the Paris Salon d'Automne: "Formerly they used to paint: I like this thing here, instead of painting: here it is" (to Clara Rilke.)

A secret drama, of which neither of them was perhaps aware, must have been enacted between the painter and the poet, a silent struggle for equality in the name of the "ultimate" that could be said, a striving by both of them for expression and representation which could not be realized in the lifetime of the artist. That explains what Rilke said to Frau Kippenberg: "She is the only dead woman who troubles me." On November 20th, 1907, Paula Becker died at the age of 31 when giving birth to her only child. This death was never directly mentioned in any letter of this period, but in various passionately tormenting meditations on death in general, the grief it caused was expressed all the more violently.

Almost a year after the catastrophe, on October 31st, 1908, the poet was surprised by lines suddenly coming into his mind, which in three days' work he was able to arrange into a requiem for his friend:

> I have dead, and I used to let them go
> and was surprised to see them all so cheerful,
> so soon at home in being dead, so right,
> so unlike their reputation. You alone
> return; brush past me, move about, persist
> in knocking on something so that it may sound
> of you and betray you . . .

Finally he succeeds in representing himself, in answering the challenge of that portrait and interpreting for his friend her life and her death with a certainty that does not recognize the being-out-of-the-world of the deceased. The life of an artist who has perished because of the contradiction between "life" and "art," yet whose achievement was "pure progress." Her "beholding" is praised and moreover, in a language that does not seek to deny the influence owed to Cézanne, there is a reference to her recklessly daring self-portrait showing the upper part of her body naked:

> And finally you saw yourself as a fruit,
> withdrew yourself out of your clothes and carried
> yourself before the mirror, let yourself in

up to your gaze; which remained, large, in front
and did not say: that's me; no, but: this is.

The main motifs in Rilke's teaching about life which has now
become almost rigid like a dogma are introduced, especially that
message of the *individual* death and the doctrine of woman's
immense capacity for feeling which far surpasses anything that
man has and which is here equated with the artist's spiritual
progress.

The tragedy of this woman's life like that of every great
woman, as the poet sees it, lies in man's inadequacy, which is
a grotesque but dangerous obstacle on the edge of woman's
course. That is why the gentle, firm voice can break out into
cutting accusations:

> For already this suffering has lasted far too long,
> and no one's learned it; it's too hard for us,
> the confused and confusing suffering of false love,
> that, building on prescription like a custom,
> calls itself right and prospers through unrightness.
> Show me a man who has a right to possess.
> Who can possess what does not retain itself,
> but only blissfully catches itself now and then
> and throws itself up again like a child a ball?

And Rilke puts it forward as an obligation that love should
not be possessive: for the sake of perfection of feeling love
should renounce the beloved who has given rise to precisely
this feeling:

> For this is guilt, if anything is guilt,
> not to increase the freedom of a love
> with all the freedom one can lay one's hands on.
> The only thing we have, where we love, is this:
> to release each other; for to retain each other
> comes easily to us and requires no learning.

The poem was published in 1909 together with a second
requiem which according to Rilke's words came to his mind so

quietly on the same current and was written on November 4th and 5th. It was for Count Wolf Kalckreuth, a young poet, who had taken his own life at the age of 19 in October 1906. The last line especially has become famous: a gnomic verse which, so Gottfried Benn said as an old man, had been the guide for his generation:

Who talks of victory? To endure is all.

PARIS AND RODIN

FOR twelve years Paris was for Rilke the geographical center of his life where, more than anywhere else, he lived and met his destiny. Although he may have gone away for short, long, or very long periods of time, he always came back there, and every arrival meant for him the equivalent of a plunge into an element of the most intense "reality" which at one and the same time was wearing and most productive. What in August 1902 was chiefly intended as a new stage in his apprenticeship, dedicated to Rodin, soon proved to be a visitation of the utmost importance, and this visitation in the course of time turned into "home": "home" in the sense of an ideal, authoritative world responding objectively to all the dimensions of his inner life.

The hopes which the young poet had placed in a meeting with Rodin were not disappointed. The old master as a living figure seemed to correspond exactly to the image they had had of him in Worpswede but at the same time to surpass it enormously. A letter to Clara Rilke written on September 2nd, 1902, describes the first visit to the studio in the rue de l'Université: "went there on the Seine. He had a model. A girl had a small plaster object in her hand and he was scratching away at it. He

Auguste Rodin.

stopped working, offered me a chair, and we began to talk. He was kind and gentle. And I seemed to have known him always. As if I were just seeing him again; I found him smaller, but yet more powerful, more kindly and sublime. This forehead, the way in which it is related to the nose, which comes out of it like a ship out of harbor . . . there is a style of stone in this forehead and nose."

About a characteristic gesture, a revealing word spoken by the master: "Then he went on working and asked me to have a look at what was in the studio. There is not a little. The *Hand* is there. *C'est une main comme ça* (he said and moved it with

such a powerful gesture as if he were holding and shaping something that one thought one could see objects growing out of it.)
—*C'est une main comme ça, qui tient un morceau de terre glaise avec des* . . . and, pointing to the two figures united in such a wonderfully profound and mysterious way: *c'est une création ça, une création* . . . It was wonderful how he said that . . . The French word had lost its gracefulness and did not take on the dull clumsiness of the German word: *Schöpfung* . . . it was detached, ransomed from every language . . . it was alone in the world:

création . . .

This is what he wrote about his first stay in Meudon in the Val Fleury, where Rodin had his villa, and which was twenty minutes by train from the Gare Montparnasse: "it is incredible what is to be seen there—just everything. *La Prière* in marble: plaster casts of almost everything. —Like the work of a century . . . an army of work. There are huge glass cases quite full of wonderful fragments of the *Porte de l'Enfer.* It is indescribable. For yards on end there are only fragments, one after the other. Figures in the nude the size of my hand and larger . . . but only parts, hardly one is whole; often there is just a piece of arm, a piece of leg, as if in motion, and a fragment of the body that belongs to them. Once there was the torso of one figure with the head of another pressed against it, with the arm of a third . . . as if a terrific storm, some unprecedented destruction, had passed over these works. And yet, the closer one looks, the more deeply one feels that, if the single bodies were whole, it would all be less of a whole. Each of these fragments is of such an eminently moving unity, so possible on its own, so without any need of completion that one forgets that they are only parts and often parts of *different* bodies which so passionately lie there against one another. One feels suddenly that it is really for the scholar to grasp the body as a whole—and rather for the artists to create new combinations out of the parts, new, larger, legitimate unities

. . . more eternal . . . And this richness, this infinite, lasting invention, this alertness of mind, purity and vehemence of expression, this inexhaustibility, this youth, this awareness that something, the best, has still to be said . . . that is unparalleled in the history of man. Then there are tables, turn-tables, chests of drawers . . . covered all over with tiny pieces—golden-brown and ochre-yellow made of baked clay. Arms no bigger than my little finger but with such life that it makes your heart beat faster. Hands which a small coin would cover and yet full of knowledge, defined quite exactly, and yet never trivial . . . as if a giant had made them immeasurably large: that is how this man proportions them."

For five years Rodin was the poet's admired model. He embodied in his eyes the idea of "greatness" in the sense of an unbroken intensity of production, an unsurpassed vitality,

Rodin's studio in Meudon.

indeed, of the creative principle in general, and in this sense his existence was a human analogy to the existence of nature. He represented the whole. ". . . what are all periods of rest, all the days spent in the woods and by the sea, all those attempts to lead a healthy life, and all the thoughts about this: what are they compared to this wood, this sea, this indescribable composure in his eyes, or to the sight of his health and confidence. His powers throb as they stream into one, bringing a *joie de vivre*, a will to live which I never imagined. His example is quite unrivalled, his greatness rises before one like a tower quite nearby, and with it all, his kindness when it appears is like a white bird circling in the light until it comes down trustingly on one's shoulder. He is everything, just everything."

These words were written in a letter to Clara Rilke dated September 20th, 1905. The monograph on Rodin about which the poet had gone to Paris was published as early as 1903; later it was enlarged by the inclusion of a lecture delivered in 1907, and new editions appeared frequently until it finally found a place in the fourth volume of the collected works of 1927. This *Rodin* of course is anything but a critical examination of a sculptor who would today be called an impressionist; it is a work in imaginative prose about Parisian artistic circles in general seen under the influence of Rodin, and it is Rilke's first prose work of any importance. Without any consideration of differences in time, style, and subject, the work of his contemporary is placed side by side with that of classical antiquity in the Louvre and the sculptures in medieval cathedrals: everything belongs to the same time and is absolutely present in a world the essential dimension of which is space. Everything is in the act of assuming form, human longing and fear. Between the old, the oldest and the new there exists unbroken continuity. There one is aware of the fear and ardor and religious striving, the medieval spirit expressed in stone: "And it was just the same with the beasts which stood and sat on the cathedrals or crouched under the consoles, stunted, twisted, and too sluggish to bear any weight. There were dogs and squirrels, woodpeckers and lizards, tortoises, rats and snakes. At least one of every species. These animals seemed to have been caught out in the woods and the paths, and because they had to live among stone tendrils, flowers, and leaves, they themselves had been slowly transformed into what they now were and were destined to remain forever. But animals could also be found who had been born in these petrified surroundings and could not remember any other existence. They had completely become the denizens of this upright, towering, soaring world. Under their fanatical leanness were Gothic arched skeletons. Their mouths were wide and screaming like pigeons, for their hearing had been destroyed by the bells nearby . . . And whoever looked at these figures felt that they were not the creation of some fancy or of some playful attempt to find new, unheard of forms. Necessity had created them. Fear of the invisible, judgments of a severe faith had made men take refuge in this visible world, and they had fled from uncertainty to this realization."

But here and now was the objectified expression of the spiritual world lying between Ibsen and Maeterlinck; with its modern complications it has been more and more scared back into the invisible: "And now? Had not a period come again which demanded this expression, this strong and forceful interpretation of the qualities inside it which were confused, enigmatic, and could not be told? The arts had somehow renewed themselves, zeal and expectancy informed them; but could it possibly be this very art of sculpture, then still hesitating in the fear of its great past, which was to be destined to find what the others were groping and longing for? It had to help a period which was tormented because all its conflicts lay in the invisible."

Some masterpieces from Rodin's studio, *The Man with the Broken Nose,* the *Porte de l'Enfer,* the huge *Balzac,* are recreated at length in words and represented with poetic imagination, not as acts of subjective consciousness but as phenomena confronting the senses. What this grand old man does has the quality of a natural phenomenon and yet it is "made," "created by skill," the uninterrupted expression as an object of that self-forgetful and restless energy: "One day the secret of this great artist's greatness will be recognized: that he was a worker whose only longing was to enter—entirely and with all his power—into the humble and hard existence of his tools. That meant a kind of renunciation of life; but it was exactly this patience which gave it to him: for the world came to his tools."

The word "work" best characterizes the chief effect the sculptor had on the poet. It contains a critical objection to the popular notion of inspiration and also a sharp criticism of the poet of *The Book of Hours*. As Rodin would have seen it, *The Book of Hours* is formless, endless, a loquacious "improvisation." "I could have gone on writing this kind of poetry forever." Work signified renouncing the wild ecstasy of feeling, ruthlessly condensing the material, strengthening the contours, concentrating intensely on the ever increasing demands of form.

The passionately sober principle of unceasing work has to be taken together with the emphasis on the "thing" when one tries to understand how Rilke was thinking in his middle period. The two together gave rise to a third: the concept of the "real." Works of art should be so real that they could rank with things in nature. The artist here made the claim not just to create something real, but to get to the root of reality, to testify that the world is real. The world, so it seemed, was not any more given without question, its reality had to be fought for and asserted every day. Against whom? Against what power? Rilke's reply anticipates a word which was to conquer the general consciousness and become uncannily popular only decades later: the word "*Angst*" (fear). In a letter to Lou on July 18th, 1903, he found as a definition of his poetic task the formula which

81

represents a wholly new horizon of feeling and thinking: to make things out of fear.

The Rodin theme as expressed in these few words had been united with a second: the Paris theme, as the poet experienced it in the very first days after his arrival and then ever more strongly until at times it caused him almost unbearable suffering: as a place of fear, poverty, and death. When, at the beginning of his notebook, the hero of Rilke's novel expresses his horror of this city in short, hard sentences, this passage is probably intended to be taken as an undeciphered confession of the author; even the details of the date (September 11th) and the room (rue Toullier) are autobiographical: "People come here then to live? I should rather have thought that they came here to die. I have been out, and I saw hospitals. I saw a poor fellow stagger and fall. People gathered round him: so I was spared the rest. I saw a pregnant woman. She dragged herself heavily along a high, warm wall, now and again groping for it as if to assure herself it was still there. Yes, it was still there; and behind it—? I looked for it on my map of the city: Maison d'Accouchement. Right. They will deliver her; they can do that."

Then too, the first Paris letters frequently expressed a melancholy which seemed almost to outweigh the happiness of his meetings with Rodin: "This town is very large and full to the brim with sadness" (to Clara on September 11th, 1902). But quite soon afterwards, in a letter to Arthur Holitscher on October 17th, 1902, he said: "I intend to stay for the present in Paris, just because it is difficult."

The letter to Lou which has already been mentioned compares his experience in Paris with the "Military Academy": ". . . just as then a great, fearful astonishment came over me, so once again I was attached by all the terror of what in some unspeakable confusion is called life." But even now this Paris was anything but a place to "dislike." It was a school of misery, presenting a challenge to the powers of feeling, seeing, and representing that could not be refused. To survive it, to respond with a Job-like effort of the heart, was a most profound satisfaction, giving austere happiness to the artistic consciousness. The letter contains a series of studies in linguistic precision which can be identified as immediate preliminaries to some famous episodes in *Malte:*

"I came to Paris in August last year. It is the time when the leaves in the city are withered without autumn, when the burning streets, which the heat has stretched, won't end, and you walk through smells as through many sordid rooms. I went past the long hospitals whose doors stand wide open with a gesture of impatient and greedy compassion. The first time I came by the Hôtel-Dieu, an open carriage was just driving up with a man lolling inside it, swaying with every movement all askew like a broken marionette, and with a heavy ulcerating tumor on his long, gray, hanging neck. And what people I have met since then, almost every day! stumps of caryatids upon whom all suffering, the whole structure of suffering was laid, beneath which they lived slowly like tortoises. And they were passers-by among other passers-by, alone and undisturbed in their fate. You caught them as impressions at most and you regarded them with a quiet objectivity like a new kind of animal, for whom misery had fashioned special organs, organs of hunger and dying. And they suffered the drab, desolate sham-life of these hypertrophied cities and endured beneath the foot of each day that trod on them like tough beetles, they dragged on as though waiting for something, twitched like chunks of a great chopped fish, already going rotten but still alive. They lived, lived on nothing, on dust, on soot, and on the dirt of their skins, on what the dogs let fall from their mouths, on any senselessly pillaged thing that might yet be bought for some inexplicable purpose . . .

"Then there were old women who set down a heavy basket beside some buttress in the wall (quite small women whose eyes were like dried-up puddles), and when they reached out for it again a long rusty hook slowly emerged from their sleeve instead of a hand, and went directly and surely towards the handle of the basket. And other old women who wandered up and down with the drawer of an old bedside-table in their hands, and showed everybody the twenty rusty knitting needles rolling about inside it, which they had to sell. And once, later in the autumn, a little old woman stood beside me one evening in the light of a shop window. She stood quite still, and I thought she was absorbed as I was in looking at the articles on show, and scarcely heeded her. But finally I felt disquieted by her presence, and I do not know why, but I suddenly glanced at her worn, oddly clasped hands. Very, very slowly an old pencil, long and thin, pushed its way out of these hands, it grew and grew, and it was a very long time before it was entirely visible, visible in all its wretchedness. I cannot tell what it was that was so frightful about this scene, but I felt as though a whole destiny were being enacted before me, a long drawn destiny, a catastrophe which fearsomely increased up to the moment when the pencil grew no longer and stuck out softly trembling from the loneliness of those empty hands. I realized at last that I was supposed to buy it."

The letter also told the story of a sufferer from St. Vitus's dance who, after a desperate resistance, had an attack in the middle of the street. This too was to find a place in *Malte*. Shortly before the imaginary drafting of a letter drawing the moral conclusion from all the horrors that had been experienced and, moreover, with a turn which no longer made it possible to distinguish the moral of loving self-sacrifice in the sense of Christian pity from the moral of *artistic* sacrifice:

"Do you remember Baudelaire's incredible poem 'Une Charogne'? It may be that I understand it now. Apart from the last stanza he was right. What could he do when that happened to him? It was his task to see in this terrible occurrence, which was only in appearance repulsive, the living spirit relating it to all

84

life. There can be no selection and rejection. Do you believe it was chance, when Flaubert wrote his *Saint Julien l'Hospitalier?* It seems to me that this was the decisive thing: whether one can bring oneself to lie down beside the leper and warm him with the heart that is warm from nights of love—that can only have a good ending."

After seven months in Paris Rilke's strength was exhausted. In order to regain his health, he fled to the seaside; from March 23rd to April 28th, he stayed in Viareggio. Here within a week he wrote the whole of the third part of *The Book of Hours, The Book of Poverty and Death,* consisting of 547 lines. It is the first work which seeks to master his Paris experiences, with artistic means which still belong to yesterday but with a subject which begins to point forward to *Malte.* That which in the first two parts was given the name of God, "the deep essence of things," is now found in fear and in misery; all the attributes of human distress are contained in the sacred name. Here too it is not deliverance from evil that is preached but surrender to evil. That is why Christ is passed over in silence and the book concludes with earnest homage to the holy poverello, who is here praised for glorifying poverty and is called poverty's great evening star, St. Francis of Assisi. What characterized him was an infinite capacity for feeling, which rejected nothing, stopped nowhere, and so could transform terror-ridden cities into the paradise of poverty. Here for the first time, with great emphasis and in a central position, a motif was developed which reappeared again and again in different connections and in different mythical ciphers.

But the story of this motif reaches its highest point only in 1922 with the *Sonnets to Orpheus.* They are one song of praise to the mangled and dismembered savior of a feeling cosmos; in Orphic language "singing" and "hearing" are used. This Orpheus is none other than the pagan counterpart to the Francis of *The Book of Hours.*

On May 1st, 1903, the poet was back in Paris. He remained for two months, and then spent the middle of summer in Worpswede and Oberneuburg, preparing there for a lengthy stay in Rome which Rodin had urgently advised for him and especially for his wife. From now on he was to be traveling about for many years and the problem of a "home" and congenial surroundings which rarely ceased tormenting him was to be solved only for a few months at a time. In his life there was a constant tension between two contrasting inclinations: on the one hand, the longing to be settled among people and close to nature, and on the other, the imperious necessity to be alone and secluded, to have strict independence, indeed no roots at all. On the one hand the room in a Paris hotel, in the rue Toullier, the rue de l'Abbé de l'Epée, later in the rue Cassette, the rue de Varenne, or in the rue Campagne-Première; and on the other, the dream of inheriting an estate, with a country house and garden, the quiet, congenial, "world of children, women, and old people," as Rudolf Kassner has put it so well.

The stay in Rome—from the beginning of September 1903 to June 1904—was not favored by good fortune like many former and many later encounters with Italian landscapes, culture, and customs. Although he managed to rent a quiet and beautiful studio, "my little summer house in the grounds of the villa Strohl-Fern," Rilke felt unable to work, suffered from ill-health, and found the city obtrusive, loud, glaring, and too pompous. In his Easter letter to Lou he wrote: "Yesterday there was a recital of Palestrina in St. Peter's. But it was no good. Everything is lost in this arrogantly large empty house, that is like a hollow doll out of which a dark, giant butterfly has crawled."

In a later letter to her (May 12th, 1904), a lengthy letter of complaint about Rome, he laid the blame for his sorry condition on the climate: "The autumn here was bad, the winter oppressive with the sirocco blowing frequently and a lot of rain, and the spring, so highly praised by everybody, is only a rush into the dangerous summer like an unbroken fall."

One can understand the strong pull of the North which the poet felt in view of a season which could not be called "spring" but a "spring exhibition": "Flowers come out and leaves, anemonies blossom and wistaria, and over and over again one says that to oneself as to someone hard of hearing. But it is all so delusively blind and superficial; there are indeed colors, but they all lie sluggishly within a cheap range of tints and do not develop from deep within themselves ... And the skies, in which there are such cheap displays of color, are flat and as if choked with sand; they are not everywhere, they do not play around things like the sky of the marsh, the sea, and the plains, they are not the infinite beginning of vast spaces but a conclusion, a curtain, an end—and behind the last trees, which stand flat like stage scenery on this indifferent photographer's sky, everything comes to an end."

Finally a polemical summing up: "And one can understand so well the empty life of this decayed people, the language of the epigones, d'Annunzio's poetry which is like garden flowers."

During these months Rilke had begun to learn Danish in order to be able to read Jacobsen and Kierkegaard in the original. On February 8th he had put the first lines of *Malte* down on paper and begun to write the story of a soul whose Danish origin and childhood perished in Paris. His imagination was full of Nordic life and culture, his mind longed for the "North, vast space and wind." And then he had a stroke of luck. Ellen Key, a Swedish governess and interpreter of the woman's movement, the author of a book on *The Century of the Child* (1902), with whom he had for some time been conducting a lively correspondence, had given lectures in her native country and in Copenhagen about his work and secured for him a series of invitations. Rilke did not hesitate for a moment to accept them and to leave Rome. On June 24th he was in Copenhagen, on the

25th in Malmö, the next day in Flädie in the Swedish province of Schonen, where they were expecting him at the beautiful, large, mansion-like farm of Borgeby-gard. He remained as guest of the owner, Miss Hanna Larssen and her future husband, the ruddy student, poet, and artist Ernst Norlind; a series of long, happy letters in fluent narrative vein to Clara Rilke told of the activities that summer in the house and the grounds, in the stables and the meadows, with trees, flowers, and animals, with abundant rainfall and a wind blowing from afar, and of the gay time spent with his new friends. He enjoyed to the full the natural healthfulness of this barefoot way of life, and showed a deep and sympathetic understanding for the peasant foundations upon which there rose "the colonnades of a refined understanding, feeling and knowledge." Here, among the young owners of the manor, the zoology student Holmström, but especially with Hans Larsson, a professor at the university of Lund, who came from peasant stock, he found an inner confidence which seemed to be the most agreeable and convincing answer to his eternal and insidious questioning about the right way to live. He spent the greatest part of autumn in Jonsered near Göteborg with the Gibson family, friends of Ellen Key. At the beginning of December he was back in Copenhagen, and on December 8th he traveled to his family in Oberneuland by way of Hamburg.

He returned from Sweden with very little in the way of poetry, but with a rich harvest of images, memories, and unforgettable moods, which later, in those periods of spontaneous productiveness, were to find expression, especially in *Malte* and in *New Poems*. 1905 did not have a promising beginning: he was beset with a feeling of perplexity and confusion. There was great uncertainty about his material future and his stagnating output. Another illness made him enter the Weisser Hirsch Sanatorium near Dresden where he spent several weeks in March and April. There he met the beautiful Countess Luise Schwerin (1849–1906), whose friendship and help was to be an influence far out-

Borgeby-gard.

lasting her premature death. In midsummer 1905, after staying in Berlin, Worpswede, and for some days with Lou Andreas in Göttingen, he enjoyed the hospitality of the Schwerins on their estate of Friedelhausen near Lollar in Hesse, met there the scientist and philosopher Jacob Baron Uexkül (1864–1944), the son-in-law of the countess, and discussed with him a plan to give an entirely new direction to his life by the systematic study of natural philosophy. At that moment an invitation reached him from Rodin to come and live for a time in his house in Meudon, in order to attend to the master's correspondence as a part-time occupation. Rilke was delighted by the invitation and was back in Paris on September 12th.

The employment, which was thus signed and sealed and corresponded roughly to the position of private secretary, lasted for almost eight months. Rilke drew a monthly salary of 200 francs but was free to interrupt his work at frequent intervals and to undertake short and also longer journeys, especially lecture tours in Germany. During this period he also returned twice to Prague, the second time in order to bury his father, who had died on March 14th, 1906. This intimate contact with his landlord and employer increased his relish for life and seemed to be a never-ending occasion for joyful admiration and productive inspiration. However, tension could not be avoided since secretarial work which, it had originally been agreed, should have taken two hours daily, devoured whole days and the poet felt his independence was being threatened. Not wishing to abandon the master, who had just fallen ill, he decided not to leave him before the autumn of 1906, but the break came on May 12th after a violent scene. Rilke suddenly found himself "driven out like a thieving servant" (to Rodin on May 12th, 1906). He took his belongings back to Paris to the rue Cassette, but was subsequently not to deny the great teacher of this middle period. The proof of this is the dedication at the front of the Second Part of *New Poems,* which runs "A mon grand ami Auguste Rodin." Only many years later, at a time when a new crisis was causing him great suffering about an unpredictable turn in his fortunes, did he write critically of Rodin also: "I have gone through so much bewilderment, experiences like finding that Rodin, in his seventieth year, has simply gone to the bad, just as though all his unending work had never been; that some niggardly thing, some tenacious trifle such as he must have kicked from his path by the dozen in earlier days, not giving himself time to finish them off properly, has lain in wait for him and wantonly overpowered him, and now makes his old age more grotesque and ridiculous every day—what am I to do with such experiences?" (December 28th, 1911, to Lou).

At first, after parting company with Rodin, Rilke could not go on living for long in Paris either. After a short journey through Belgium he stopped at Godesberg, Friedelhausen, Berlin, and Munich. At Wacholderhöhe, a country house near Godesberg, he was received by a new admirer and Maecenas who had been one of Countess Schwerin's circle of friends and had already made his acquaintance in the previous year: the banker and writer Karl von der Heydt (1858–1922). Just a short time before that he had succeeded in attracting a wider public for Rilke's lyric poetry by a careful review of *The Book of Hours* in the *Preussische Jahrbücher*. He and his wife Elizabeth were the persons to whom the first part of *New Poems* was dedicated; as a token of gratitude for a sympathy and active help which was to prove quite indispensable as time went on, and above all in those late years in Paris. But in the autumn of 1906 provision for the poet's material conditions of life and work was not secure, and the problem of where he was to spend the next winter was causing acute embarrassment. The solution came once more from

Rilke and Clara, 1906.

the Schwerin circle: Frau Alice Faehndrich (1857–1908), a sister of the countess, invited him to spend the next months at her villa Discopoli on the island of Capri.

He arrived on December 4th and was given the Rosenhäusl, a pretty secluded studio in the garden of the villa. In the evenings they all assembled for conversation in the small domestic circle. Later, in spring, they embarked on joint work: the mistress of the house, the daughter of an English mother, gave him each day the preliminary translations of the *Sonnets from the Portuguese* by Elizabeth Barrett Browning and Rilke responded with poetic versions of the sonnets which are one of his most impressive acts of homage to woman.

All kinds of lyrical work were written, dedications, experiments, a seven part cycle "in honor of Saint Mary of Cetrella," and other things; this precocious spring drew from him joyful letters of celebration, the most beautiful of which are addressed to Clara Rilke. What was denied in Rome three years before was granted in full measure here: that "sea morning," spring on the southern island which was for the poet, just as it had once been for Goethe, a substitute for the glory of the Greek world which he had never seen with his own eyes.

On May 31st, after short stays in Naples and Rome, Rilke was back in Paris, and now, suddenly, this city which had most sorely tried his will to endure had transformed itself into a place of blessing, a true home. The following months were so fruitful that later he called them the happiest in his life. This joy was the result of a laborious ripening process which grew more acute from one crisis to another and of prolonged patience with himself. Now, finally, the poet was in a position to come before the public with a book which for the first time deserved the honorable title of masterpiece. *New Poems* appeared in December 1907. They contained works from the years 1903 to 1907, and, above all, almost the whole production of the years 1905 and

1906. The earliest piece is the famous *Panther*, the latest, the third poem of the Insel cycle (August 1907).

With this volume the history of German poetry was enriched with a new type of lyrical expression: the so-called *Ding-Gedicht* (objective poem) which Rilke created and can only be explained from his special development; it had already reached the highest pitch of perfection imaginable in his work. It is the fulfillment of the program "to make things; not sculptural, but written things—real things, proceeding from the craftsman's hands," as he once put it, under the keen impression of Rodin's creative power, in a letter to Lou (1903). The process of creating motifs has changed fundamentally since the phase of *The Book of Hours*. No longer is that general outpouring of feeling which has been aroused by "life" and its attributes God, love, and death the occasion for the lyrics, but the clearly defined and strictly separated figure: works of art, animals, plants, characters from history, legend or biblical tradition, and also travel impressions and town views (Furnes, Brussels, Ghent, Rome), and static, calm situations and impressionistic images in which some feeling suggested by the world is presented like an object without any sighing or screaming. Everything that Rodin showed him or enabled him to understand could be a model for him to test his linguistic powers on as he appropriated and transformed it: the antiques in the Louvre, the Winged Victory of Samothrace or the famous Attic relief, the Orpheus with Eurydice and Hermes, the capitals and rose windows of Chartres, the botanical and zoological world of the Jardin des Plantes. He persisted in remaining "in front of the motif" until it surrendered, "in front of nature." The use of words like "present," "real," "necessary" becomes a kind of mania in these years. Does he not work like an artist? Like a sculptor? But, in addition to single figures, which seem to transpose a marble statue into language with a sublime and fanatical accuracy, like the introductory and motto poem "Early

Rilke in the Hôtel Biron.

Apollo," there are others such as "Last Evening," "Eranna to Sappho," "David Sings before Saul," "The Lace," which are highly imaginative and contemplative. Phenomena from quite different areas and forms of existence of reality are made of one and the same fundamental matter, pervaded by one and the same meaning, for there is only one criterion for what is real: "that it is present like feeling." This is the explanation for the simultaneity of all the figures and situations, the simultaneity of "Morgue" and "Early Apollo," of "Joshua's Council," "The Merry-Go-Round," and "The Steps of the Orangery."

"To learn how to look" (the task Rilke gave himself when he left for Paris) thus means basically to intensify to the highest pitch the awareness of how the world can be felt, to intellectualize and objectify the Chopin-like sensibility there is in one's nature. What "Panther," that brilliant success of a poet only twenty-seven years of age, achieves is not just "intuition" but identification of ego and thing, objectivation of feeling.

Kassner has remarked that with Rilke "intelligence is deposited or formed around feeling." That is exactly what Malte is thinking of when he says of Abelone, the mysterious female figure of his childhood: "it is however possible that Abelone tried in later years to think with her heart."

MASTERPIECES OF A NEW ART

THE virtuoso-like certainty in the use of his own artistic resources, which the poet had fought for and achieved by about 1907, the realization of the Rodinesque *"toujours travailler"* in the solitude found so conducive to work, the well-tempered equilibrium of wanting to and being able to, of planning and doing: this mostly blessed state continued after *New Poems* for about another three years. At the end of 1908 there followed *New Poems: Second Part*, a collection of lyrical masterpieces in which the artistic formula of Rilke in his middle period seemed to have ripened into a perfection that could not be surpassed. In June 1910 the *Notebooks of Malte Laurids Brigge* appeared. Only with the conclusion of this experiment in prose was the fruitfulness of this harvest exhausted, and a new agonizing crisis of expression began.

The letters of these years, chief among which are the famous Cézanne letters to Clara Rilke written in October 1907, have a tone of sovereignty and calmness. As Rilke pays tribute to the mighty painter (who died in 1906) and to the glory of his incessant *"réalisation,"* he always speaks indirectly and sometimes even directly about himself and his own inner way "to an absolute happy and elemental productivity which can now scarcely again be exposed to any outside threat" (to Anton Kippenberg, March 11, 1908). And what is quite different from years ago when he met the father gods Tolstoy and Rodin, he can ask himself the question: "To what extent has that development been already realized in me which corresponds to the immense progress in Cézanne's paintings?" (October 11, 1908).

The Salon d'Automne that year had a magnetic power of attraction for the liveliest minds in Paris. Germany too sent some most distinguished visitors, men like the dazzling critic Meier-Graefe and Count Harry Kessler, one of the most important connoisseurs and collectors of his time. Rilke paid an almost daily visit to look at the pictures which seemed to have created during these weeks a new concept of painting—in spite of van Gogh or, it could be said, as a final confirmation of van Gogh—, and almost every day he sent his wife an account of what he had seen. On October 7th, 1907: "You know at exhibitions how I always find the people walking around so much more remarkable than the paintings. That is also the case in this Salon d'Automne, with the exception of the room where the Cézannes are. On the one hand everything is reality: there is this dense, wadded blue of his, his red and his shadowless green and the reddish black of his wine bottles. How feeble all his objects are too: the apples are all cooking-apples, and the wine bottles are intended for bulging old coat pockets. Farewell."

Rilke sought information about the life and behavior of his hero. In something like twenty letters he wrote his monograph, an imaginative account of Cézanne: the figure and the fate of an old man who went his way, poor and ill and lonely, pursued by children who threw things at him. His morose taciturnity, his madness, his innocent fits of rage quite fascinated the poet: "In the evening when he gets back home, he is annoyed by some change, grows angry, and finally when he notices how exhausted that makes him, promises himself: I'll stay at home; and work, just work."

For a long time now he could not find any model, he worked from old drawings, which he had made forty years ago in Paris: "'At my age,' he said, 'I could at most get a woman of fifty, and I know that such a person could not be found in Aix.' So he painted from his old drawings. And placed apples on bedspreads which Madame Bremond must certainly have missed one day and put his wine bottles among them and anything else he happened to find. And (like van Gogh) he made his 'saints' from such things; and forced them, *forced* them to be beautiful, to represent the whole world and all its happiness and glory, and did not know if he had persuaded them to oblige him. And he sat in the garden like an old dog, the dog owned by this work which called him and beat him and starved him."

A rigorous monism of art was proclaimed here, a sanctification of the productive effort, which had driven out or absorbed in itself all the non-aesthetic values of the human soul and in so doing had drawn very close to inhumanity: ". . . his mother he loved too, but when she was being buried he was not there. He happened to be '*sur le motif*' as he called it. Even in those days

97

Self-portrait of Cézanne, 1890–1894.

his work was so important for him and brooked no exception, not even one which his piety and simplicity must surely have recommended" (October 9th).

Rilke in his interpretation of Cézanne identifies himself radically and categorically with the idea of "*la poésie pure*": "The good conscience of these reds, these blues, their simple truthfulness teaches you; and if you place yourself among them as receptively as you can, they seem to be doing something for you. Also you notice, better and better each time, how necessary it was to get beyond even love; it comes naturally to you to love each one of these things if you have made them yourself: but if you show it, you make them less well; you judge them instead of saying them. You cease being impartial, and love, the best thing of all, remains outside your work, does not enter into it, is left over unresolved beside it: this is how the sentimentalist school of painting came into being (which is no better than the realist school) . . . This consuming of love in anonymous work which gives rise to such pure things, probably no one has succeeded in doing so completely as old Cézanne; he was supported in it by his sullen and mistrustful inner nature" (October 13th).

In order to check his own impression, in order to have confirmation from an eye feeling exclusively as a painter, that he had not judged too subjectively and "distracted by literary elements," he asked the German artist Mathilde Vollmoeller, then living in Paris, to accompany him to the exhibition: "But imagine my astonishment when Fräulein V., trained and using her eye wholly as a painter, said: 'Like a dog he sat in front of it, and simply looked without any nervous or irrelevant speculation.' And she said something else, very good in connection with his technique (which you can see from an unfinished picture). 'Here,' she said, pointing to the spot, 'he knew what he wanted and said it (part of an apple); but there it is still open, because he didn't yet know . . . He only did what he knew, nothing else.' 'What a good conscience he must have had,' I said. 'Oh yes, he was happy somewhere right inside him' " (October 12th).

But it was precisely this absolute agreement of the painter's eye with the poet's which seems to prove that the poet's mind was to press forward to a new understanding of itself, that it was setting itself aims which were substantially different from what was understood by poetry in the classical literature of Europe. If, from Plato to Hölderlin, it had been regarded as credible that there was a "God," dwelling in the poet and inspiring his poems so that the poet was nothing but the mouthpiece of this God, here, in Rilke's middle period, the poet is expressly placed on the same level as the "artist," and the latter is to be compared not to a God but to a dog. Furthermore, everything which the old European notion of poetry embraced, such as doctrine and example, meter and law, political and rhetorical education, religious and moral constraint: all that is removed, and what remains is an ideal of purely artistic perfection. To the poet the crucial matter is by practice in looking and studies in precision to refine and differentiate the instrument of language beyond anything that had hitherto been possible.

His ambition is to describe a self-portrait in such a way that no detail goes unseen (October 23rd), or, as it were, to rival with his prose the well-known picture of a lady in a red armchair so that the painterly and the linguistic forms entirely coincide: "In this red armchair, which is *personality,* a woman is seated, her hands in the lap of a frock with broad vertical stripes. The frock is done quite lightly in little scattered dabs of greenish yellow and yellowish green up to the edges of the blue-green jacket, which is held together in front by a blue silk bow shot with emerald. In the brightness of the face the close proximity of all these colors serves as simple modeling; even the brown of the hair curving around the head and the smooth brown of the eyes have to assert themselves against their surroundings. It seems that each part knows of all the other parts. So much does it participate in them; so much proceeds from their harmony or discord; so much does each, in its own way, care for the balance and produce it: just as ultimately the whole picture holds the reality poised. For if you say it is a red armchair (and it is the first and last red armchair of all painting), it is only because it binds up with itself an aggregate of sensed colors which, whatever else they are, fortify and confirm its red. In order to reach the height of its expression the chair is painted quite powerfully round about the delicate portrait, so that something like a coat of wax has arisen; and yet the color has no ascendancy over the object, which seems so perfectly translated into its pictorial equivalent that, finely as it is caught and rendered, its bourgeois reality loses all its heaviness in its ultimate picture essence. Everything . . . has become an affair of the colors among themselves: one masses itself against the others, emphasizes itself with reference to them, broods on itself alone. As in the mouth of a dog at the approach of certain things various fluids form themselves and hold themselves in readiness:—affinitive ones which only assimilate and corrective ones which seek to neutralize—so, inside each color there occur concentrations or dilutions by means of which it overcomes the touch of another" (October 22nd).

The lyric poems of these years were frequently written as a response to works of modern painting. Twice it was a Cézanne which served as model: *The Abduction* and *The Temptation,* and twice a Manet: *The Balcony* and *The Reader.* Corresponding to the "Early Apollo" in the first part of *New Poems* is the "Archaic Torso" at the beginning of the second part; its model is the early Greek statue in the Louvre known as *The Torso of a Youth from Miletus.* The last poem of the volume is the reproduction as a lyric of a figure of the Buddha which had been seen in Rodin's garden: "Buddha in Glory." Even where he chose quite independent subjects, Rilke liked to assume the figure of a portrait, for example, in "Portrait of a Lady of the Eighties" or in the poem entitled "Portrait" dealing with the figure and the fate of the great Eleonore Duse.

Culture is everything: even landscapes are interpreted as cultural phenomena in the poem which is so very often art conscious and makes the artistic act absolute. But it is remarkable how this poet is fascinated by a city as a work of art, an achievement like Venice, for example, in which the will of so many generations which was creating culture appears, as it were, capitalized. "Late Autumn in Venice," dating from the early summer of 1908, is one of the most brilliant contributions made by German lyrical poetry to the image of Venice and sums up the quite unconventional feelings which the author had experienced in the city on the lagoon during a stay of eleven days. On the recommendation of Meier-Graefe, he had been invited to the house of the ladies Nana and Mimi Romanelli, sisters of high birth, whose hospitality had been especially memorable and indeed captivating because of young Mimi's beauty. A correspondence was begun and lasted for some years with a considerable and often rapturous display of feeling.

The numerous but mostly brief travels of this phase of Rilke's life had nothing of the questing and often tormented restlessness of some earlier and some later periods. There was something light-hearted and carefree about them because the poet is quite sure about this homeland of his choosing and spends much time agreeably indoors. The destinations were those that have already been mentioned: Oberneuland, Berlin, Munich, Prague, Rome, Venice; and he made a stay of six weeks on Capri, in the spring of 1908. Among the new friends

Les Baux.

of these years the publisher Anton Kippenberg (1874–1930) and his wife Katharina became more and more prominent. He frequently made their beautiful house his destination, finding its "tower room" an ideal retreat: it was there that the final version of the *Malte* novel was prepared for the printer at the end of February and the beginning of March 1910. Two journeys to the South of France opened up for him sunny Provence (May 25th–30th, 1909) and memorable Avignon (September–October 1909). He saw Arles and Orange, Les Baux and Tarascon, and the famous Saintes Maries de la Mer with all its churches.

About Les Baux he wrote: "Have you never heard of Les Baux? The approach is from Saint-Remy where the soil of Provence grows nothing but fields of flowers, and suddenly everything changes to stone. A completely denuded valley opens, and scarcely is the hard road inside than it closes in behind; three mountains are thrust forward, sloping mountains propped

Avignon: the Papal Palace.

up one behind the other, three springboards, as it were, from which three last angels leapt with a terrified bound. And opposite one, inlaid far away in the sky, like stone in stone, rise the edges of the strangest settlement, and the way to it is so barred and obstructed (nobody knows whether by debris from the mountains or a tower) that one thinks one is going to have to fly up oneself if one is to reach that open void up there with body and soul. That is Les Baux. That was a fastness with houses round it, not built but dug into the limestone strata, as if men driven by a stubborn desire to have a dwelling had found room there like the drop from the eaves which at first rolls away when it falls but persists and finally lives with its fellows and remains" (October 23rd 1909).

A permanent record of the imaginative writing that resulted from these travels is to be found above all in the last passages of *Malte*. The hero's fantasy is kindled by the past, he tries his hand at reproducing historical events in writing, and it is almost as a matter of course that "Avignon" fits into the mosaic of childhood memories, Paris experiences, and the "reminiscences of his reading."

"Les Alyscamps" (Elysian Fields) is the name of an avenue of ancient tombs which every visitor to Provence must have seen. In Rilke's case the sight of them must have been felt immediately as a challenge to his creative powers, as a motif of a superior order which could not be exhausted in a single period of activity. But almost thirteen years were to pass before he could finally make use of this unique memory. The tenth poem of the first part of the *Sonnets to Orpheus* is dedicated to it.

With the completion of *Malte* Rilke has covered the range of subjects belonging to those great years spent in Paris and created a counterpart in prose that is equal in quality to *New Poems*. He has given to the world a work which one day will rank with all those great masterpieces which represent some breakthrough. This book is an early, exemplary attempt to ask and answer questions that will later return with the authors of existential philosophy and in the popular literary form of existentialism, especially the question: "How is it possible to live if the elements of this life are completely incomprehensible to us?" Almost contemporaneous with Kafka's *Penal Colony,* the book makes a daring advance with a frank analysis of *Angst,* thereby recording the appearance of a new phenomenon in the world: "The existence of the horrible in every particle of air! You breathe it in as something transparent; but inside you it condenses, hardens, assumes pointed, geometrical forms between your organs. For all the torments and agonies wrought on scaffolds, in torture chambers, madhouses, operating rooms, under the vaults of bridges in late autumn: all these have a stubborn imperishability, all these persist, and, jealous of all else that is, cling to their frightful reality."

Angst is to be understood as the pitiless loss of all inner points of security save one: the strength of a consciously trained sensibility capable of dialectical acts of "turning." "Only a step," says Malte, "and my deep woe would be beatitude."

Throughout his life Rilke insisted that it would be wrong to identify him with his hero; he has rejected as improper "all attempts to exploit *Malte Laurids Brigge* as a mine of biographical material" (in a letter to R. H. Heygrodt, December 24th, 1921), and has always emphasized a feeling of critical detachment when he discussed the fate of "poor Malte."

The trial which Malte could not survive, the author himself, it seems, did survive by the very writing of this book, by succeeding in objectifying these despairing confessions of his second self. With the completion of the *Notebooks* he created for himself a foundation for future progress. It was in this brisk and confident tone that he wrote to Kippenberg on March 25th 1910: "Now everything can really begin. Poor Malte at the outset is plunged deep in misery and reaches, one may say, eternal bliss; his heart covers a whole octave: after him now almost all lyric poems are possible."

But the new beginning was slow in coming and the Malte who had supposedly been overcome clings like a hungry jackal to the author's heels and for a long time would not let go. Almost two years after sending the manuscript away he was to ask himself whether the imagined downfall of his hero had not after all exhausted him more than he had been willing to admit at the time. ". . . no one but you, dear Lou, can distinguish between us and show whether and to what extent he looks like me. Whether he, who is in part compounded of my own dangers, perishes in order to keep *me,* as it were, from perishing; or whether I have only now, with this *Notebooks,* really got into the current that will sweep me away and dash me to pieces. Can you understand that this book has left me stranded like a survivor, my soul in a maze, with no occupation, never to be occupied again? The nearer I approached the end the more strongly did I feel that it would mean an indescribable cleavage, a high watershed, as I always told myself; but now it is clear that all the water has flowed towards the old side and that I am going into a parched land that grows no different. If this were all! But the other one, the one who perished, has somehow used me up, has defrayed the colossal expense of his ruination with the strength and the objects of my life. There is nothing that was not in his hands, in his heart, he appropriated everything with the fervency of his despair; hardly does a thing seem new to me when I discover the fault in it, the jagged edge where he broke off. Perhaps this book ought to have been written as one detonates a mine; perhaps I ought to have sprung away the moment it was ready" (December 28th, 1911).

DUINO, AFRICA, SPAIN

BETWEEN the year when *Malte* was printed and 1923, when the *Duino Elegies* appeared, Rilke published a single book of his own poetry, *The Life of Mary* (1913). The process of development concealed behind this long silence did not become visible and intelligible until after the death of the poet: as a result of the publication of the numerous volumes of letters and a huge quantity of lyrics. What, after the completion of the novel, was first felt as a temporary exhaustion of his creative powers soon turned out to be a wide-ranging crisis in his life and a profound change of consciousness. Rodin's *"toujours travailler"* had exhausted its validity, the notion of form in *New Poems* had served its purpose, and the subject matter of the thing poem (*Ding-Gedicht*) yielded nothing more. "With a sort of shame," he complained in the letter to Lou which has just been quoted: ". . . I think of my best time in Paris, that of *New Poems,* when I expected nothing and nobody, and the whole world streamed towards me only as an ever greater task to which I responded clearly and surely with pure achievement. Who would have said then that so many relapses lay ahead of me! I wake up each morning with a chill in the shoulder, just where the hand ought to seize and shake me. How is it possible that, ready and trained for expression, I now remain without a calling, superfluous?"

Only very much later was there to be an explanation of the meaning of this exhaustion and loss of production. There were frequently to be other complaints about having run dry, and for many years he was tormented by an inability to produce anything deserving to be called connected work. The complete output of the years between 1910 and 1926 is however so large that it was not until 1955 that a survey was completed of the corpus of scattered poems (which had been published singly during his lifetime) and of those which were posthumous. If the chronology is studied closely, it will be seen that both before and after that glorious February of 1922 to which we owe the two main works of the late period, there were several other phases of considerable productivity, especially in the years from 1912 to 1914, then in the late autumn of 1915, and then again in the period from the beginning of 1924 to the end of the summer of 1926. In the intervening periods the poet had repeatedly had to put up with a weakening and an interruption of his creative powers, especially in the last three years of the First World War when they dried up almost completely. The chronology of the late work also reveals that the crisis of expression that began after *Malte,* insofar as it was a crisis of form and subject matter, had already been overcome by January 1912. With the two great poems which then came into being and were later to be included as the first and second in the *Duino Elegies,* there began in the poet's development a new epoch which was to be the last and decisive one. The "later Rilke" had made his appearance.

In the last four years before the outbreak of war the poet stayed in about fifty different places for a short or a longer period, so great was his restlessness and the feeling that his seclusion in Paris had ceased to be a refuge for him. He wanted to be among "people," although he knew that "things are going badly with me when I *expect* people, need people, look around for people: this only drives me still further into my misery and puts me in a false position; they will never know how little trouble I take on their account and of what ruthlessness I am capable" (to Lou, December 28th, 1911).

His loneliness had become homelessness: "You need only know what I mean by "people": I do not want to give away

108

my solitude; it is only that, if it were a little less in mid-air, if it got into good hands, it would lose its morbid undertones entirely, and I could achieve at least some kind of continuity in it, instead of being chivvied amid the din of shouting from pillar to post with it like a dog with a stolen bone" (to Lou, January 10th, 1912).

He thought of giving a completely new turn to his life, possibly of going to Munich and immersing himself in academic studies at the university, of at last filling the gaps in his education. He complained of nervous trouble ("my physique runs the risk of becoming the travesty of my spirituality"), discussed with Lou a plan to undergo psychoanalytic treatment (January 20th, 1912), but abandoned it again only a few days later: "I know now that there would be some point in psychoanalysis only if I were really serious about that remarkable *arrière-pensée* of giving up writing which since completing *Malte* I have entertained as a kind of relief. One could then have one's devils driven out, since in bourgeois life they really are only a disturbance and an embarrassment, and if the angels possibly go with them, that too would have to be taken as a simplification and one would have to say to oneself that there would be no place for them in that new profession (which?)" (to Lou, January 24th, 1912).

What is concealed in these capricious letters and their slight complacency about his own illness is the fact that the "good hands" to which his straying solitude might be entrusted had in fact already been found, and that the writer had already been privileged to enjoy for two years the succour of a new and extremely helpful friendship which in the last fifteen years of his life was to play just as decisive a role as once did his connection with Lou as a young poet. It was the friendship with Princess Marie von Thurn und Taxis, née Princess Hohenlohe-Waldenburg-Schillingsfürst (1855–1934). Rilke had met her in Paris in December 1909 when the initiative had been taken by the

109

Princess Marie von Thurn und Taxis-Hohenlohe.

princess, who had come to know of the poet's work from Rudolf Kassner (b. 1873), a member of her intimate circle. In the spring of 1910 Kassner for his part became personally acquainted with Rilke through the princess, and the result was an extraordinary, fruitful, and intellectual constellation which was of lasting importance for all three participants and was to lead to a rich literary output on all sides.

Whereas for Rilke Kassner grew more and more into the role of the only man his equal in stature, and in the eyes of the philosopher Rilke represented the phenomenon with all its problems of a completely poetical existence, for the poet the princess was not only patron, supplier of his needs, and Maecenas with considerable social power but also the most vivacious and sensitive friend and a mother figure of a unique kind. In his *Buch der Erinnerung* Kassner has paid a surpassing tribute to the human and spiritual pre-eminence of this woman: "Marie von Thurn und Taxis was first of all a great lady, this she was in the highest degree, impressing all who came close to her as such. She was born in Venice when it still belonged to Austria and was a citizen of that greater Austria which was destroyed in the World War and in spite of political unviability, perhaps for that very reason and as an attendant phenomenon, succeeded in creating more types than any other country in Europe; for anyone who saw Austria as it really was, these types were an unmistakable blessing. Her Venetian origin, together with the time she spent in her youth in Duino, Sagrado, and Tuscany, the close connection with the court of the Count de Chambord through her mother who belonged to the della Torre family which had given patriarchs to Aquilegia and a number of dukes to Milan, and also the fact that her uncle, Cardinal Hohenlohe, kept her in contact with the Rome of Pius IX, was a greater influence than was later Vienna or the "Bohemian Forest," as she liked to say. For her, Italy belonged to her memories and was not, as with other Germans, a country satisfying one's longings or offering escape. I can recall the hour when I approached the couch on which she was lying as an invalid in order to inquire about her health—it was a few years before her death—and she replied that the whole morning one single thought had occupied her mind and in that thought there had been taste, smell, feeling, recollection, longing, and bliss, everything together: the grapes in autumn on the tiled wall in Sagrado when she had been a child and with them the smell of the laurel bushes with the sun shining on them and the burning wood. It had all brought back her childhood so clearly that there had been room for only one other feeling, anxiety lest she should have to wake up and go away. 'And you see, that is happiness, real happiness. There is no other.' "

111

Rudolf Kassner. Drawing by Ernst Noeter, 1907.

This woman who was "grand" in every respect certainly admired her poet from the bottom of her heart, kept faith with him during his life and after his death wrote an intelligent and noble memoir about him, one of the finest which have ever appeared, but where necessary she could speak plainly to him and occasionally bring into play in the most refreshing manner her superiority in matters of instinct, knowledge of the world and of men. Highly comic effects could result when her sound common sense collided with the exaggerations of the Rilkean cultivation of the feelings. When the poet told her once more of the tormenting conflict one of his admirers had caused in him, one of those many gushing women who had been aroused by his words and his human sympathy and who crossed his path more frequently as he grew older, she made the following reply:

"But Dottore Serafico! *Everybody* is lonely and *must* remain like that and *must* endure and *cannot* give way and *must* not seek help in other people but in that mysterious guidance we feel within us without knowing or understanding it.

"And who can feel it as much as you, you whom the gods love but are so ungrateful! And why do you always want to rescue stupid women who should rescue themselves—or the devil take them!—he will most certainly bring them back. (You don't need to take offense, for I know nobody and know of nobody.)

"It seems to me, D. S., that the late Don Juan was an orphan child in comparison with you—and you are always looking for such mournful cases which are not nearly so mournful in reality, believe me.

"*You, you yourself* are looking for your own reflection in all these eyes" (March 6th, 1915).

Rilke, ashamed and moved at the same time, promised to behave better. "Your beautiful heavy thunderstorm" is what he called this letter in his reply.

The Taxis castles of Duino on the Adriatic (not far from Trieste) and Lautschin in Bohemia were the places where Rilke and the princess most frequently met to enjoy the friendly, sociable atmosphere of the aristocratic family: Kassner would often join them to make a third. The first stay at Duino lasted from April 20th–27th, 1910, and was followed by twelve days in Venice: this obvious combination was to be repeated several times later. In a letter to Hedwig Fischer on October 25th, 1911, the poet has described the castle which was built boldly upon a rock and was to be made famous throughout the world by his poetry:

". . . I will tell you at once where I am: with friends in this immense castle towering up by the sea and like the foothills of human existence looking out from many of its windows (among them one of my own) on to the most open waters, directly on to the universe, one feels, and its transcendent spectacles,—while inner windows on a lower level look into quiet, secluded courtyards, where in later times old Roman walls have been softened by baroque balustrades and playful figures. Behind, when one has left the safety of all the gates, there rises the empty karst which is no less pathless than the sea, and the eye, unimpeded by any triviality, is especially moved by the little castle garden which tries to creep down like the surf at the point where the castle does not occupy the whole slope; then the wild garden comes into its own, growing where the shore next juts out, and there, hollow and in ruins, lies the still older castle building which stood even before this immemorial castle; tradition says Dante tarried on its outer fortifications."

Rilke's second stay in Duino began in October 1911 and lasted, with two minor interruptions, until May 8th, 1912. This very aristocratic seat with its atmosphere nourished by the centuries could not fail to represent for him anything other than quite ideal seclusion, especially when, at this time, he was left alone with the less important members of the scattered

Duino Castle.

household. Nevertheless it was only in January that the new solitude proved productive. In the middle of that month the urge to write poetry had returned. Heinrich Vogeler, Rilke wrote in a later letter to H. Pongs, "in whose visitors' book I had occasionally written poems about the Virgin Mary while I was in Worpswede, was intending to publish this early verse together with drawings by myself. To prevent this and at least to provide him with a better and more concerned text, I wrote in a few days, consciously casting my feelings back, these poems which, but for one or two, are of little consequence; *The Painter's Book of Mount Athos* with its pictorial headings served as object reference.

Such was the genesis of *The Life of Mary,* one of Rilke's sublime parodies of figures from the passion and salvation of Christ. It is a chain of hymns to woman's primacy of feeling, a Song of Songs on the passion of his mother caused by the "man" Christ and a characteristic argument against the son and the "son's kingdom" (Kassner) in general and in favor of the Virgin Mary and the kingdom of children, women, and old people. It is, by the way, the only one of Rilke's works to inspire a congenial, complementary achievement in another art—and successfully: the music of Paul Hindemith (1923).

But writing this poetry was only the beginning of a creative movement which was unexpectedly to enable the poet to make the boldest progress and to bear him up to heights far surpassing anything he had hitherto attained. What took place during these days was not a "work" process in the sense of Rodin and Cézanne and impelled by will power, but a mysterious growth of inspiration and deepening of feeling which seemed to confirm again the old Platonic notion of the poet's "divine" mission. One day, Rilke later remembered in conversation with his Duino hostess, he had been detained indoors by a tiresome letter to which a reply was needed while outside a violent wind was blowing and the sun was shining down on to a brilliantly blue and silver sea. He had taken that letter, still unfinished, out with him and gone down to the bastions. But there, some 200 feet above the waters of the Adriatic, he had suddenly felt as if in the roaring of the storm a voice had called out to him: "Who, if I cried, would hear me among the angelic orders?" He had immediately written these words down together with some other verses which had seemed to follow of their own accord. Then he had gone back to his room and that same evening the first elegy had been finished.

With that the poet had entered the hermetic circle of a linguistic revelation which was to separate him henceforward from all his contemporaries as the chosen one who was to write the greatest lyric poetry of his time in the German language. And he had burdened his destiny with a task which would remain unfinished for more than ten years and be a heavy burden for him, making almost superhuman demands on his flagging, unresponsive strength which had been almost utterly sapped by the war and the post-war years, and representing the quintessence of all promise. He managed to complete the second elegy as well in January and in the first days of Febraury 1912. The beginnings of the third, the sixth, the ninth, and some other fragments came to him, but above all the powerful first lines of the tenth:

> Some day, emerging at last from this terrifying vision,
> may I burst into jubilant praise to assenting angels.
> May not one of the clear-struck keys of the heart
> fail to respond through alighting on slack or doubtful
> or rending strings! May a new-found splendor appear
> in my streaming face! May inconspicuous Weeping
> flower! How dear you will be to me then, you Nights
> of Affliction! Oh, why did I not inconsolable sisters
> more bendingly kneel to receive you, more loosely
> surrender myself to your loosened hair? We wasters
> of sorrows!

But that was all for the moment; the creative movement had come to a halt. It was only in the late autumn of 1913 that new lines came into being, and again two years later, in November 1915, when a new elegy, the fourth, was added to what existed already. Then there was more silence and no productivity for more than six years, a dreadful price to pay for the future completion of the whole.

All the motifs which occur in the first two elegies are already familiar to us from earlier works. What is new and overpowering is that they have been liberated from the isolation and objectifying restrictiveness of the objective poem and transformed into elements of a comprehensive interpretation of human existence in general, a large-scale song of the world which carries away all details into its elegiac-hymnic current. Just as in Hölderlin's late work, it is concern for man's *epochal situation* that constitutes the thematic heart of the whole.

An almost systematically arranged doctrine of being and living is proclaimed, a quite independent, quite personal myth, emancipated from the heritage of Western tradition, which has its own "saints," its models and protagonists: the hero, those who died young, the lovers, the angels, or even *the* angel, who represents a symbol of the supernatural and superhuman, a kind of pseudonym of God. Besides these nameless persons there are the guiding figures who are expressly canonized by being included in this definitive text. For example, in the first elegy there is the Venetian poetess Gaspara Stampa (1523–1554), whose love for Count Collalto, at first unrequited and finally going beyond the husband and being directed to the infinite, radiates a fame which even today is undiminished. What Rilke is celebrating in his poem is a counterpart, with a shift in meaning, of the cosmos of the Christian-Western tradition: hierarchically ordered between beasts and angels, but taken quite "inwardly," a world made entirely of feeling, triumphing in the invisible. In the all-embracing unity of this spiritualized cosmos the boundary between life and death has lost its validity and ceased to be the opposite of immanence and transcendence. Being is pure im-

117

manence: "world-inwardness," feeling and capable of being felt. This stretches to the farthest limits of the universe and has taken, so to speak, into itself the mysteries "God" and "Death."

There is a new law-form corresponding to the new, greater thematic matter: the vast-arching rhythm, the rhymeless long line, the freely running meter with a Germanic-classical feeling. The "French" ideal of form seems no longer to be a compelling force, the German classical models become more attractive, and Rilke finds himself in involuntary agreement with an elegiac-hymnic tradition reaching from Klopstock through Goethe and Hölderlin down to the present day. Now was the time when he discovered Goethe, whom he had ignored for so long and to whom he had still shown hostility in *Malte* because of Bettina (who loved in vain). In December 1913 he read the whole of Kleist. Hölderlin had a still greater influence upon him, especially the poet of the late hymns and fragments which had of course remained hidden for more than a century and had been discovered only a short time before the First World War and brought to the notice of the public by the George disciple Norbert von Hellingrath (1888–1916). Rilke had made the acquaintance of the young scholar in Paris as early as 1910 and followed his work for many years with the keenest interest. How these most advanced achievements of German poetry must have delighted him, how perfectly did that law of form as formulated by Von Hellingrath under the words "rough arrangement" agree with his own visions of form! The special volume on Hölderlin published in the summer of 1914—an advance printing from the fourth volume of the Hellingrath (provisional) collected edition—could not have had a more reverent reader than the poet of *Duino Elegies,* and everything that was written in the first months of the war bore the traces of this reading. Not least was the poem addressed to Hölderlin himself and dating from September 1914, one of the most magnificent tributes among the poems inspired by Hölderlin in the language of the twentieth century that we know.

The two most important journeys during these years were the one to North Africa (from the end of November 1910 to the end of March 1911) and the other to Spain (November 1912 to February 1913). It was only after some hesitation and then a very sudden decision that Rilke embarked on the African enterprise, being influenced especially by the need to get as far away as possible from *Malte,* Paris, and his own irresolute and ailing condition. Algiers, Biskra, El Kantara and Carthage were the first places he visited. On December 17th he was in Tunis, on the 21st in Kairuan, a "holy city," like Mecca, in Islam: "It is wonderful how one feels here the simplicity and vitality of this religion. The Prophet seems to have lived yesterday, and the city is his like a kingdom" (to Clara Rilke, December 21st, 1910).

At the beginning of January he left Naples on the second stage of his journey: first to Cairo, then up the Nile past Memphis and Thebes, Luxor and Karnak to Assuan. On January 18th, 1911, he wrote from Luxor to his wife: "On the eastern (Arabian) bank to which we are moored is the temple of Luxor with the high colonnades of pillars with lotus buds. Half an hour farther on this incredible temple world of Karnak which I saw the very first evening and then again yesterday just as the moon had begun to wane and could not take my eyes away—good heavens! one concentrates and looks intently, full of a desire to believe, yet one's gaze passes over them (only a god can command such a field of vision). There is a chalice-like pillar, a sole survivor, and one cannot take it in, it means more than this life, and it is only when night comes that one grasps it somehow, putting it on the whole with the stars, from them it becomes for a second human, a human experience. And just imagine that yonder in a westerly direction above the two

119

Karnak: columns of the temple of Ammon.

arms of the Nile and the fertile land the Libyan mountains can be seen, lovely in the desert light; today we rode through the huge valley in which the kings lie at rest, each of them under the weight of a whole mountain, on top of which the sun leans heavily, as if no force could hold kings down."

On February 10th he was back in Cairo, feeling that he

had overtaxed his strength: "Cairo is three worlds with which one has to cope," he writes to Kippenberg, "one just doesn't know how to get through it all: there is a vast city spread out remorselessly, there is all the Arabic life, so dense that it becomes opaque, and behind it, eternal, restraining, and warning, there stand these inexorably large objects of Egypt" (February 10th, 1911). When he fell ill, he was rescued by the German Baron Knoop (who had already been helpful in the winter of 1907 as host to Clara Rilke), and invited to spend several weeks at his house in Heluan. On March 29th he returned to Venice, tolerably restored to health.

Rilke's premonition that many and tremendous impressions of Egypt would be there to be dealt with later, perhaps much later, proved to be correct. It was once again that great productive state of intoxication occurring in February of 1921 in which all the essential memories came crowding together, and with other parts of the world the African scene too was caught by the poetic current and recorded. The whole of the second part of the tenth elegy, perhaps the most magnificent vision that Rilke ever imagined, might be understood as a poetic transformation of an Egyptian landscape, especially of that "huge valley in which the kings lie at rest." The poet himself has referred to the Egyptian worship of the dead in order to explain the thought content of the elegies, but felt obliged to add: "At the same time the 'Land of the Threnodies' through which the Threnody Elder conducts the young man who has just died is not to be identified with Egypt, it is only the reflection, so to speak, of the Nile country in the desert-like clarity of the dead man's mind" (to Witold Hulewicz, November 13th, 1925).

When, two years later, Rilke traveled to Spain, he was spiritually much better prepared than when he left for North Africa: a long-standing wish was being fulfilled. The letters he wrote from Toledo, Cordoba, and Ronda show that he was

Toledo. Painting by El Greco. Metropolitan Museum, New York.

strong and calm and in full possession of his imaginative faculties. From Toledo he wrote to the Princess: ". . . a town belonging to heaven and earth for it is really in both, for it passes beyond all being. I tried recently to make it intelligible to Pia in a single sentence by saying that it existed equally for the eyes of the dead, the living, and the angels . . . This incomparable town has difficulty in keeping inside its walls the arid, undiminished landscape, the hill, the pure hill, the hill of the apparition—the earth as it leaves it is enormous, and immediately outside the gates it becomes world, creation, mountains and ravine, Genesis" (to Marie Taxis, November 13th, 1912).

Like all newly discovered towns and landscapes during his life, the Spanish scenery too comes to correspond objectively to inner states, moods and advances in his intellectual development. It is remarkable that it was to be Spain, that most "Catholic" of all countries, which was to make him formulate his aversion to the Christian religion which had been growing for years with a severity never experienced hitherto. He said in a letter from Ronda: "Moreover, you must know, Princess, since I was in Cordoba I have become an almost rabid anti-Christian; I am reading the Koran—in places it strikes a chord in me and I echo with all my powers, like wind in an organ. Here you are supposed to be in a Christian country, well, here too it has long been overpassed,—it was Chrstian so long as you had the courage to kill somebody a hundred paces outside the town, where the innumerable unassuming stone crosses flourish on which stands simply: Here died so-and-so—really they ought not to sit any longer at this denuded table and dole out the last remaining finger-bowls for food. The fruit is sucked dry —all that is left for us is, speaking crudely, to spit out the rind. And yet Protestants and American Christians *will* go on making a brew of this weak tea that has been drawing for two thousand years—the next to come was in any case Mahomet; like a river bursting through a mountain he bursts through to the one God, who can be gloriously apostrophized every morning without the aid of the telephone 'Christ,' where all the time you bawl 'Hello, who's there?'—and no one answers." (Ronda, December 17th, 1912).

The sympathy for Islam which he had already felt in Kairuan had thus become still stronger in the meantime. Religion —as his faith in the "whole," in the miracle of world-inwardness demanded—should not depend on belief, salvation, and a mediator. For him religion meant inward-being, a relation

123

"without an opposite," in other words a religion of the "people" or the "blood." Even later therefore, after the completion of the *Elegies,* he was emphatic that the angel in them should be thought of as "bearded" and must not be confused with the notions of Christian tradition. "The angel of the *Elegies* has nothing to do with the angel of the Christian heaven (rather with the angelic figures of Islam)" (Hulewicz, November 13th, 1925).

What is characteristic for Rilke's development is the "self-will" which remained unbroken even in times of crisis, that continuous agreement with himself, that consequent and completely undiverted self-unfolding of a very personal range of subjects which can already be recognized in the poems about angels and girls of 1898. With reference to his early attempts he could say: "I do not deny them, but it seems to me as if what I had to say was so very much one thing and always this one thing, that what later replaced them was simply expressed better and more maturely and so they only represent provisional drafts in relation to the definitive versions" (to St. Zweig, February 14th, 1907).

Even when he translated—and in the pre-war years he translated a good deal and with eagerness in order to occupy his formative powers when his talent was unproductive—his subject remained with him. After completing the German version of the Barrett Browning sonnets he translated another three important documents on the history of the power of woman's love: an old French sermon which is attributed with some probability to Bossuet (1627–1704): "The Love of Mary Magdalene" (1912); then the "Portuguese Letters" of the nun Marianna Alcoforado (1640–1723), which are among the most famous love letters in world literature (1913); finally "The Twenty-Four Sonnets of Louïze Labé of Lyons, 1555" (1918). Was not this gallery of great lovers, whose unrequited feelings seem to go beyond the bounds of all human comprehension, his own completely personal discovery and did not his conception of world-inwardness and indeed his own personal notion of reality stand and fall with the credibility of their martyrdoms?

Among the important women of his time there was one especially that corresponded exactly to his notions: Eleonora Duse (1859–1924). He sought and obtained her friendship; he was with her almost every day in the summer of 1912, which he spent as the guest of the Princess Thurn und Taxis: ". . . as you can imagine we were like two people coming into action in an old mystery play, spoke as in the recitation of a legend, each one his gentle part. A meaning emanated from the whole and instantly passed out beyond us" (to Marie Thurn und Taxis, July 12th, 1912).

And yet it was precisely in these meetings with the Duse that it was seen how little Rilke's respect for women's greatness was a blind ideology, and how much during those years his pronounced sentimentality revealed a necessary reverse side: a no less developed feeling for the grotesque: "Now she wears herself out, maltreating her own body . . . In September she wanted to come back here, but the house she has in mind has not been found, also half an hour is sufficient for her to wear an apartment out, even the ceiling can't be used any more. A distaste for living issues from her in certain moments which is so piercing that it shakes the teeth out of everything in her vicinity."

He was also busy translating a find from the nineteenth century: *The Centaur* by Maurice de Guérin (1810–1839), and André Gide's *Return of the Prodigal Son,* a subject which had already engaged his own attention in *Malte.* The exchange of views with Gide (1869–1951) whom he had first met in 1910 was one of the most agreeable human relationships during his later years in Paris. Gide for his part translated passages from *Malte* into his own language, and of the leading French authors of that time he was the one to show the liveliest interest in

125

Eleonora Duse.

everything German: "Gide knows enough German for it to be possible to examine single passages with him, it was fine and productive and I could imagine that my work had closely reflected the meaning of his book."

And there was something much more astonishing to report. "Just imagine what I discovered in Gide's excellent library—you won't guess: Grimm's big dictionary. I happened to be in search of a certain expression and spent hours with it (to Anton Kippenberg, February 3rd, 1914)."

Other members of this Paris circle were Romain Rolland, the witty Comtesse de Noailles ("that fierce little divinity"), and the Belgian poet Emile Verhaeren. Altogether Rilke, in spite of his growing admiration for Goethe and Hölderlin, remained throughout his life an attentive and even passionate observer and connoisseur of contemporary literature. Thus it happened that he was one of the first to read Marcel Proust and recognize his extraordinary significance, and this as early as 1913!

THE WAR

ALL those subtly branching international relations which bound Europe's finest brains together, all the loftier achievements, plans, and hopes were suddenly and brutally interrupted by the outbreak of war. Rilke happened to be in Germany when the catastrophe broke. He had been the Kippenberg's guest in Leipzig for a week and on August 1st he arrived in Munich to consult the neurologist Dr. Freiherr von Stauffenberg. The immense patriotic enthusiasm that accompanied mobilization worried him more than it excited him, and yet, in some remarkable way, he suddenly felt he could respond with poetry. The *Five Songs,* which were written in the early days of August, are the only lyric "document of the times" that we have by him, and it is certainly no exaggeration to say that they are the most important imaginative work in the German language which that unhappy event has produced.

At that moment when even Hofmannsthal and Schröder broke out into patriotic oaths and wrote conventional songs of defiance, Rilke had the courage, the strength and the far-sighted accuracy to glorify not war but pain.

The "legacy" of Hölderlin profoundly inspired an elite of German university students and many endeavored to interpret the tremendous event, the war, with the pure, ardent thought of this poet. In the circle of Rilke's friends and acquaintances too there were a number of highly gifted young men of this kind, and not a few of them were destined to share the fate of an early death. The artist Götz von Seckendorf fell as early as 1914, the poet Bernard

127

von Marwitz in 1918, Hellingrath, and the highly gifted Franz Marc (whose paintings had become an "event" for Rilke) were killed in 1916 in the battle for Verdun.

Rilke spent by far the larger portion of the war period in Munich. All in all they were gloomy years and produced little in the way of poetry. The exultation of the *Five Songs,* this hymnic expression of a universal emotion, had passed all too quickly for him as for all the nations involved, and never returned. In the summer of 1915 he wrote to the young Frenchwoman Marthe Hennebert, a protégé from his years spent in Paris: "You will believe me when I tell you that for a year I have been dragging myself step by step through a desert of pain and bewilderment; I suffer and that is all, I lack the slightest relief from any activity for I could only fight for all and not against anybody. Will any God ever have enough balm to heal this enormous wound which is what the whole of Europe has become?"

Life itself with all those natural things which gave it meaning seemed to have lost its force in those years. When the princess wrote him a few hasty lines on a cheerful postcard thanking God for the still intact condition of Duino castle, he replied on a note of poignant melancholy: "For me your letters belong to the very, very few things which signify some continuity of the past with the future, I hold on to them as it were to look ahead—if only I knew to what. That I did not write is due to the reserve and moroseness of my nature from which I can extract nothing except anxiety or lamentation, and I cannot pass them on to you! Nor is there any sense in telling you how pleased I am that Duino has remained in good condition so far, for . . . meaning will only return to our joy, hope, and suffering when life has once again become more comprehensible and more human for us . . . (September 6th, 1915). Duino was later almost completely destroyed by artillery fire.

Only relatively little travel, two periods undergoing treatment in Irschenhausen in the Isar valley (August–September 1914 and February 1915) and six months in Vienna, interrupted his uneasy residence in Munich. The poet visited Berlin almost annually, although its loud and energy-charged atmosphere was much less salubrious for him than the calmer and more civil mood of the Bavarian capital. He went to Vienna in December 1915 in order to do military service. Although he had been declared unfit after a medical examination in May of that year, bureaucracy acted again a few months later and was much harsher this time. On January 4th he had to report for military duty and suffered a period of three weeks' infantry training in barracks. At the end of January he was sent to the army record office: "There my position (office hours from nine to three) is outwardly more comfortable and a change for the better, but it is probably untenable if I do not succeed in being transferred to quite mechanical copying or recording work; for the kind of writing these gentlemen have been practicing for the past eighteen months I find quite impossible. I just do not wish to describe it, it is very miserable and ambiguous, and a cessation of all intellectual activity (as was the case in the barracks) seems enviable compared with this crooked and irresponsible misuse of writing. These gentlemen themselves call it the "beauty treatment for heroes," it made them shudder for a long time, but now they have overcome that and just scribble it down. There will certainly be many difficulties—for the moment they don't know what to do with me and keep me in that state of utter idleness which is one of the most striking military experiences" (to Kippenberg, February 15th, 1916).

He characterizes his mood perfectly in a single sentence: "I taste in myself, when I try it for a moment, nothing but patience, patience with no admixture, pure colorless patience."

On June 9th, as a result of friends' intervention, he was released from his unpleasant situation and handed his discharge papers. He remained for some weeks in Rodaun near Vienna and here he had his portrait painted by Lou Albert-Lasard, an artist

Hugo von Hofmannsthal.

and friend he had known in Paris, Irschenhausen, and Munich. The presence of Hugo von Hofmannsthal who had a baroque mansion in Rodaun is noticeable as a beneficent influence: "You must know, princess, how nice and agreeable both the good Hofmannsthals are as neighbors: they are in two ways, one, because we are living in the old-fashioned Stelzer inn, and then because we really work in the little arbor facing the Hofmannsthals and can use the garden belonging to it where peonies and roses are now opening, catching up with one another" (July 2nd, 1916).

On July 20th he returned to Munich and went to live again in his hospitable and shady house in Keferstrasse immediately adjoining the English Garden.

If one disregards the first weeks after the outbreak of war, only a single phase can be recorded during these years in which that inner numbness relaxed and the poetic springs began to flow again: the late autumn of 1915. Not only was the whole of the fourth elegy written, but also a series of extraordinary fragments and sketches, a masterpiece like "The Death of Moses," and the brilliantly audacious poem "Death," in which we have the grotesque counterpart of the "intimate" idea of "one's own death." And the elegy written on November 22nd and 23rd has a mournful, Novemberish tone. Even the meter—the iambic pentameter—distinguishes it from most of the other Duino elegies which are written in hymnic-dactylic, agitated measures. Of all the elegies it is the most bitter, expressing the melancholy side of the late Rilkean doctrine of life. The theme is the tragic insecurity of man in contrast to all natural life, plant or animal:

> O Trees of life, what are your signs of winter?
> We're not at one. We've no instinctive knowledge,
> like migratory birds. Outstripped and late,
> we force ourselves on winds and find no welcome
> from ponds where we alight. We comprehend
> flowering and fading simultaneously.
> And somewhere lions still roam, all unaware,
> while yet their splendor lasts, of any weakness.

The boldly shortened introductory line seems to conjure up a moment just before winter beneath leafless trees, perhaps during a walk through a Munich park: trees are aware of their winter but human beings are not aware of theirs. What would be called "freedom" in idealistic and also in Christian-dogmatic language is in Rilke's eyes complete unnaturalness and hopeless ambiguity:

> I will not have these half-filled masks! No, no,
> rather the doll. That's full. I'll force myself
> to bear the husk, the wire, and even the face
> that's all outside. Here! I am sitting on.

In a visionary image-language in which autobiographical reminiscence and daring speculation mutually penetrate one

131

another with a hermetic, enigmatic effect and with a compelling, almost cogitative consequence which succeeds once again in achieving the lofty style of Kleist's *Marionettentheater,* the drama of human consciousness is evoked:

> ... when I feel like it,
> to wait before the puppet stage, —no, rather
> gaze so intently on it that at last
> a counter-poising angel has to come
> and play a part there, snatching up the husks?
> Angel and doll! Then there's at last a play.
> Then there unites what we continually
> part by our mere existence.

This fourth elegy, like all the others among the ten, acknowledges the anti-Platonic and anti-Christian fundamental emotion of Rilke's "metaphysical" poetry. In those years the poet has insisted more and more resolutely on abolishing the difference between nature and freedom. Man must turn to nature, must be merged with it, the two becoming one substance.

What the poet said about the war in a retrospective letter dating from 1920 applies almost exactly to the following years: "Practically all through the war years, *par hasard plutôt,* I was waiting in Munich, always thinking it must come to an end, understanding nothing, nothing, nothing! *Not understanding:* that, indeed, was my sole occupation, and I can assure you that it was not easy! (to Leopold Schlözer, January 21st, 1920).

Rarely was Rilke so receptive for outside influences than at this time when his own creative nature was so seriously troubled and hindered. Reading inevitably became one of his chief activities. Hölderlin kept him busy for a long time, then there was Tolstoy, Hamsun, a book like Gundolf's *Shakespeare und der deutsche Geist,* and, as always when his own work was not going too well, the need arose once more to undertake regular "studies." Among the new influences to which he opened his mind the archeologist and student of the mysteries Alfred Schuler deserves special mention. Schuler (1865–1923) belonged with Klages and Wolfskehl to that group of Munich cosmologists which had been formed from the circle around Stefan George. He was an admirer and pupil of the Basle jurist and student of myths, Johannes Jakob Bachofen (1815–1887) and owed a great deal to his doctrine of maternal law. In the Munich of the war years his lectures on Roman antiquity and especially on the attitude to life and the cultural customs of the late imperial period caused great excitement and much controversy. The "pagan" moods animating these cosmologists found a suggestive expression in the powerful eloquence of this man; Klages called him a new embodiment of unextinguished sparks of the distant past, and he himself later gave instructions that he should be buried in Roman costume.

Rilke had already heard him in 1915 and made his personal acquaintance: ". . . just imagine that a man with an intuitive insight into ancient imperial Rome undertook to give an explanation of the world which represented the dead as the real

Munich: 11 Keferstrasse, the house in which Rilke lived from autumn 1915 to summer 1917.

beings, the world of the dead as a single incredible existence, and our own brief span of life as a kind of exception to it: basing all this on a tremendous width of reading and such a depth of inner conviction and experience that the meaning of the most ancient myths, made manifest, seemed to flood into this river of words, bearing the meaning and the conviction of this strange eccentric on its strong current . . ." (to Marie Turn und Taxis, March 18th, 1915).

This spontaneous acquiescence and agreement with Schuler's line of thought is not a surprise. Rilke's idea of a world of space, his passion for the "open" as the unity of life and death could nowhere have found more intense confirmation than in the lectures of this self-willed mystagogue.

Rilke always drew to himself and absorbed only those elements from his spiritual environment which were homogeneous and congenial and were able to confirm his own understanding of the world. Almost simultaneously with Schuler's influence an ever growing interest in the doctrine of Sigmund Freud is seen in the letters and poems. In Rilke's eyes it was one and the same principle of reasoning which held good in Schuler's world of tombs and Freud's monism of the sexual: renunciation of the Christian hereafter, of Christian spiritualism and the unnaturalness of Christian morality, and the recognition of a single here and now enlarged by the world of the dead. Even before the war he had thought of exposing sexual mystery: ". . . this laying bare of the secret that is a secret through and through, on every spot, that there is no need to hide it. And perhaps everything phallic (as I intuited in the temple of Karnak, I could not think of it at that time) is only an exposure of the human "private secret" in the sense of the "open secret" of Nature. I cannot bring to mind the smile of the Egyptian gods without the word "pollen" occurring to me . . ." (to Lou, February 20th, 1914).

Among the rough drafts of the late autumn of 1915 there are also seven poems glorifying the human phallus, the figurative language of which ignores the most delicate taboos of European society and transgresses so unhesitatingly all bounds of taste that more than forty years passed before anyone dared to publish them. (They were printed for the first time in the second volume of the collected works in 1956.) The act of physical love is blasphemously celebrated here in religious metaphors, and, in places, in notions from the Christian story of salvation. Here deep feeling, the sense of world inwardness is experienced as the intoxication of the sexual embrace: the womb of the beloved is space, universe, "heaven."

In a short prose work dating from February 1922 Rilke has developed in detail his thought on the revelation of human sexuality and drawn positive consequences from the reflections set in train by Schuler and Freud. This "Young Worker Letter" joins in the anti-Christian hymn to the glory and power of the "here and now" which Nietzsche had been the first to sing forty years before: "What insanity to side-track us towards a Beyond, when we are here surrounded by tasks and expectations and futures! What treachery to purloin the images of actual delight so as to sell them behind our backs to Heaven! O it is high time the impoverished earth collected all those loans we have raised on its splendor, in order to furnish something 'beyond the future with them.'"

But the essence of earthly splendor is sex, our "lovely" sex, that force which Christianity has held in suspicion for two thousand years, concealing it—and here occurs the key word of psychoanalysis—"repressing" it: "And here in that love which, with an insufferable mixture of contempt, lasciviousness, and curiosity they call 'sensual,' here are to be sought probably the worst effects of that degradation Christianity thought fit to wreak on the earthly. Here everything is distortion and repression, although we proceed from this deepest of occurrences and ourselves possess in it the center of all our transports."

Freud's doctrine of the sexuality of the child is quoted, and a

135

kind of psychoanalytic criticism of culture is hinted at. In his speculating passion the writer goes so far as to consider a deification of sex possible, if not to demand it, that is, to refer to this center of our power of feeling and imagining the God-creating powers of the human soul which have ceased to be bound for a long time now: "Why did they make our sex homeless for us, instead of transferring thither the whole festival of our birthright? Good, I will admit that it ought not to belong to us, who are unable to accept responsibility for such inexhaustible bliss and control it. But why then do we not belong to God from that very spot?"

That Rilke was far from being Freud's disciple or follower is proven not only by the last sentence but by the whole text. He has never taken over ideas from other authors without involuntarily transforming them until they became his own, without converting them to his own needs. Thus here he has reshaped a medical discovery into poetical myth: the shepherd god Priapus takes the place of the displaced, spiritually misunderstood Christ. All the same, peace has been made with psychoanalysis even if he continues to resist its practical therapeutic claims. On December 29th, 1921, he wrote to Lou: "Are you in Vienna, dear Lou? Then give Freud my kind regards—; I rejoice to see that he is now beginning to have considerable influence in France which has so long been deaf."

When the war ended, Rilke had made little progress with his work, and the fragmentary and disjointed condition of what he had written must have depressed him more than it had four years earlier. But his destiny was work and not people, those many persons who managed to win his affection and whom he spoiled with his letters, letters about which Kassner has said: "The work and the letters are like the coat and the lining, but the latter is made of such costly material that one day someone will hit upon the idea of wearing the coat with the lining turned outside." As regards the persons, especially the women who were caught in the wake of his sensitive originality, he himself has most strongly characterized his relation to them when he said: "Of course they cannot know how little trouble I really take with them, and how ruthless I can be." But such words tell only half the truth. According to Kassner, he was the absolute opposite of the dilettante or wastrel and therefore did not seek out the so-called handsome woman or demand or even recognize her but felt "woman from the woman's point of view." Rilke again and again experienced from the passionate bestowal of women's affections the most intense feeling of which man is capable and that stimulus of his own genius, but this was then inevitably followed by a relapse into the void, into a complete helplessness as between one person and another. That applies for example to his relationship with the pianist Magda von Hattingberg (1913/14) who has taken her place in literature under the name of Benvenuta:

"What finally made me so completely wretched began with many, many letters, which were so facile, so beautiful, dashed down from the heart; I can hardly remember ever having written the like . . .

". . . as if I had come upon a new and full gushing forth of my innermost being, which now, released in inexhaustible messages, poured forth in this gayest affection, while I, in these daily letters, felt both its happy current and that enigmatic restfulness which seemed the most natural thing to expect in a recipient."

And the end: ". . . three months of undone reality have laid something akin to a stout plate of cold glass on top of it, beneath which everything is as unpossessible as in a museum showcase" (to Lou, June 8th and 9th, 1914).

He wrote in quite similar terms, but a few months later, a summary of his relationship with Lou Albert-Lasard, "my friend Lulu": "How much and whether, if only just a little, she will be able to be one of your daughters, cannot be foreseen, but if it were possible for you to like her, there would once again be

137

something worthwhile in her life. On the whole I did not do her any good, and after the first few weeks of giving and hoping (that is how I am), I took most back, all those recantations of my heart which is so quickly obstructed in human relationships, and now it is clear to us both that I cannot help and that I cannot be helped" (to Lou, March 9th, 1915).

The prostration of the prodigal son at the end of *Malte,* the gesture of a man who is loving and yet cannot love, is the tragically grotesque model of all these relationships: "Have I kindled such brightness in you? Such a fire in your heart? Dear child, and now you are feeling your way back to me—instead of going away into the open world into which you are surely drawn . . ." (in a letter dated December 29th, 1918, to Claire Studer, aged 21, who later married Ivan Golls).

THE LAST ADOPTED HOME

THE political events of autumn 1918, the termination of hostilities between the nations of Europe and the outbreak of the German Revolution, were greeted by Rilke with renewed confidence and followed attentively. It was not only that he could derive hope for himself and his own situation which troubled him more internally than externally. What had weighed upon him for years as a visitation and made him sterile had been precisely this universal state of distress, the catastrophic, inhuman deterioration of the spiritual climate, the senselessly repeated mass slaughter, the immense devastation. Was not the lot of this seemingly so asocial man bound up much more closely and momentously with the fate of contemporary society than was the merely rhetorical existence of certain politically committed debaters and pamphleteers who kept themselves busy in the foreground and disappeared again with the topics of the moment? Where Rilke showed some interest in politics was at those stirring turning points of history which seemed to make it possible for man to transcend his eternal moral mediocrity, but this was never at the expense of an unbiased study of the way things were really going. When in November 1918 the revolutionary movement became vocal and important in Munich too and in the Munich manner, he was seized with a feeling of liberation from political incompetence that had now had its day. Just as in August 1914 he thought he could trust the signs of a general change of mind:

"In the last few days Munich has given up something of its emptiness and quiet, the tensions of the moment make themselves felt even here, though they do not comport themselves in an exactly edifying manner among these Bavarian temperaments. Everywhere huge gatherings in the beer-halls nearly every evening, speakers all over the place, among whom Professor Jaffé is obviously first-rate, and where the halls are not adequate, gatherings under the open sky in thousands. I also was one of the thousands on Monday evening in the rooms of the Hotel Wagner. Professor Max Weber of Heidelberg was speaking, a political economist considered to be one of the best heads, and a good orator, and after him, discussing the anarchy and the wearing strain, more students, fellows who had been four years at the front, —all of them so simple and frank and "of the people." And although you sat around the beer tables and between the tables in such a way that the waitresses could only eat through the dense human structure like weevils, —it was not in the least oppressive, not even for the breath; the fog of beer and smoke and people did not strike you as uncomfortable, you barely noticed it, so important was it and so clear above everything else that things could be said whose turn had come at last, and that the simplest and truest of these things, insofar as they were presented more or less intelligibly, were seized upon by the immense crowd with heavy and massive applause. Suddenly a pale young worker rose up, spoke quite simply: 'Have you or you or you, have any of you,' he said, 'made the offer of an armistice? And yet *we* are the people who ought to have done it, not these gentlemen at the top; if we could get hold of a radio station and speak as common people to the common people over there, Peace would come at once.' I cannot say it half as well as he did, but suddenly, when he had said this, a difficulty struck him, and with a touching gesture towards Weber, Quidde, and the other professors standing on the stage beside him, he continued: 'Here, these professors, they can speak French, they'll help us to say it properly, as we mean it . . .' Such moments are wonderful, there have been all too few of them here in Germany, where only intransigence found words, or submission which in its way is only a participation in violence by the oppressed" (to Clara Rilke, November 7th, 1918).

But only a few weeks later his rising hopes had changed to disappointment and the substance of politics had been transformed back into that sorry, opaque, and morally inferior material which he knew only too well from earlier experiences: ". . . under the pretext of a great revolution the old lack of principle is at work, swaggering under the red flag. It is dreadful to say so, but there is no more truth in this than in all those calls to join the army; there was no mental integrity in either. So-called mental integrity came only after this event as well and, just as in 1914, could only 'offer its services' which goes to show that there is not much to be said in praise of mental integrity. Momentarily we are all out of breath; busy picking up peace which has fallen out of everybody's hands and broken into a thousand fragments, we have never seen it as a whole and that is just what we needed to: to see its greatness, its pure greatness after the chaotic monstrosity war was . . . And then this temptation to dabble in political dilettantism which could lead people to generalizations outside their competence and to introduce ex-

140

periments when the greatest wisdom and deliberation is called for" (to Anni Mewes, December 19th, 1918).

As for Rilke's personal situation, during these weeks he was telling everybody that he was only living for the day when he could leave Munich and how he longed to quit this city he had never liked very much. He had had to give up his nice flat in the Villa Alberti in Keferstrasse in July 1917 and had only been able to find a new place in Schwabinger Ainmillerstrasse in May 1918. He had spent the intervening months partly on the Westphalian estate of Böckel near Bieren as the guest of Frau Hertha König, a writer whom he had known since 1910, partly in Berlin (October to December), and partly in a room in a Munich hotel. As early as November 1918 he looked into a plan for a lecture tour in Switzerland, but nothing came of it. It was months later before he could really tear himself away and set out on that journey which was to end at his last adopted home. An invitation from the Hottingen Reading Circle to give a lecture in Zurich on October 27th, 1919, caused him to turn his back on his Munich room on June 11th and to leave for Switzerland, going first to Rome and then to Nyon on the Lake of Geneva where a certain Countess Dobrezensky had offered him a refuge and hospitality in her Chalet d'Ermitage. Nobody could have guessed at that moment how much, how completely, hospitable Switzerland would take him into its care, and that he would never set foot in Germany again.

In the months that followed he was frequently on the move, full of that old enthusiasm for travel—"after five years' immobility"—and in his whole body and soul there was a feeling of rejuvenation and renewal: "First, however, I had the desire to make use of my freedom and see the country, which it is true I have always in other years regarded only as a country of passage, being somewhat mistrustful of its too famous, too obvious, and too pretentious 'beauties.' Mountains, to begin with, are not very easy for me to grasp. —I managed to see the Pyrenees, the

Autumn 1917 in Böckel.

Atlas Mountains in North Africa belong to my sublimest memories, and when I read of the Caucasus in Tolstoy I felt the indescribable fever of their grandeur. But these Swiss mountains?
They still seem to me something of an 'obstacle'; there are so
terribly many of them. Their shapes rise up conflictingly; I can
make out with some satisfaction that somewhere a contour runs
pure against the sky, —but, how shall I put it? I lack the simile,
the inwardly perceptible parallel to them which alone turns an
impression into an experience. First I approached, tentatively,
the towns: Geneva (which is but a motor-drive's distance from
Nyon)—then Berne, and that was very, very lovely. An old,
settled, in some places quite unspoiled town with all the marks

of a sturdy and active citizenry, even to the high self-assurance that shows out of the unanimous-looking houses, preening themselves above their porches with an aloof air where they face the street, but towards the river Aar, with a more communicative and open mien where the lovely gardens lie outspread" (to Countess Aline Dietrichstein, August 6th, 1919).

From the end of July to the end of September he was in Soglio in the Bergell district, enjoying the atmosphere of an old palazzo belonging to the old federal family of von Salis, which had been made into a guest house.

In October a lecture tour which had been planned long ago took him by way of Zurich to St. Gallen, Lucerne, and Berne and finally to Winterthur where he won new friends in the art-loving Werner brothers, Oskar, Georg, and Hans Reinhart. Almost at the same time the bourgeois aristocracy of Basle, especially the Burckhardt family, began to show interest in him and his personal circumstances, and on Christmas Eve he received an auspicious letter from Dory von der Mühll, the sister of the historian and later minister Carl J. Burckhardt, holding out the prospect of an invitation. Rilke was very interested, seeing on the horizon a new chance for his work: "Madam, this new proposal . . . an inner voice tells me: I have my wish, I have my wish, unless it is mistaken—; but how could there be any mistake as it is Christmas?"

He confessed the secret, ever-present worry that was gnawing at his soul: "Years ago, in the winter of 1912, I did once have it, quiet, solitude, real, for four, five months, it was unprecedented. And just now I only long for one thing, to take up again those great works (as yet you don't know any of them); to do that I need inwardness and no interruption, like the rock inside the mountains when it is turning into crystal. Only yesterday I was wondering: how can I earn that from God? What does the dumb creature in the mineral do for God so that he leaves it to keep busy for years in the middle of its own law—, without disturbing it: it keeps on and on, it succeeds!" (December 24th, 1919).

But even the shelter afforded by the Burckhardt's hospitality which he enjoyed from the end of February to the beginning of June, first in the Ritterhof at Basle, and then on the family estate of Schönenberg near Pratteln, did not yet suffice to bring about that longed for contact with the one essential. The feeling of homelessness was still not exorcised, and again during the summer and autumn of this year inner unrest drove him through the whole country and twice even across the frontiers. From June 11th to the middle of July he was in Venice to meet his faithful Princess Taxis and to stay once again in the mezzanine he loved in the Palazzo Valmarana, which he had occupied during the whole summer of 1912. Finally, in October, he celebrated his return to Paris and for "eight indescribable days" he was entirely happy: "What can I say, everything is good, completely and absolutely good; for the first time since those terrible years I am feeling the continuity of my life, which I was on the point of renouncing; for even Switzerland only perpetuated (more mildly, more pleasantly, more hiddenly, if you wish) the breaks, but here, here—*la même plénitude de vie, la même intensité, la même justesse dans le mal:* apart from the political muddle, everything has remained great, everything strives, surges, glows, shimmers—October days—you know them" (to Countess Mirbach-Geldern, October 27th, 1920).

When winter was near which, the poet had firmly resolved, was to be spent working, he still did not know where he would be living; and he entertained the thought of leaving the country once more. Again the "miracle of Swiss hospitality" occurred: Frau Nanny Wunderly-Volkart, a cousin of Werner Reinhart (a member of the Winterthur circle), whom he had known since the autumn of 1919, found an ideal place for him: Berg Castle in Irchel, the property of a colonel Ziegler, half way be-

144

tween Zurich and the Rhine: "The terms were like those in Duino and that decided me. I live alone in this solid, centuries-old stone house, alone with a housekeeper, who attends to my needs in silence just as I allow myself to be attended to in silence; a forsaken park open to the quiet countryside, no railway station anywhere near and, moreover, at the moment all the roads closed because of foot and mouth disease—so *retraite absolue*" (to Marie Taxis, November 19th, 1920).

And really: the constant solitude of Berg which lasted for six whole months and was broken only once was not in vain. Numerous drafts, fragments, and profoundly tender "dedications" for friends were proof that productivity was gradually reviving. The most important thing he wrote during this winter was the great poem of childhood "Let What Was Infancy," which again reached the standard of the elegies and was also originally intended to be included in the Duino cycle. A most remarkable event occurring during the early weeks in Berg was the penning

Castle of Berg in Irchel.

of a series of poems which, Rilke often asserted, were not by him but were rather communicated or dictated to him by some strange ghostly person. One evening at the end of November, as he later narrated the incident to his publisher, "he had spoken the lines to himself as he was undressing, and among them were:

> Mountains rest, by stars illumined; —
> but as well in them there glitters time.
> O, within my wildest heart there darkens
> without a roof that immortality—

and he had said to himself in astonishment: these lines with their pathos are not yours! He had dressed again, somewhat agitated, and had sat down by the fireside. Suddenly he had seen on the chair opposite him a gentleman in old-fashioned clothes who had read aloud to him from a faded manuscript poems in which the lines had occurred that Rilke had spoken to himself. He had then copied these lines down."

That was how the cycle *From the Literary Remains of Count C. W.* came into being: a series of ten poems which were completed a few months later by an additional eleven. Since the poet could find nothing in Berg castle except Goethe's works, which might have met his need for ancestor worship, an old library, and the magic of posthumous papers, he set about—as he wrote to the princess—"writing a notebook of poems which he pretended to have found here in a cupboard, working leisurely and provisionally." Thus he "invented" this count and endowed him with his own memories, melancholy, imaginings, suggested to him the Rilke family's idiosyncrasy, and gave him his own travel experiences.

In the version supplied to Kippenberg of the genesis of this cycle, whether one regards it as a mystification, an invention, or a true account of an hallucinatory experience, there is expressed in any case a completely disinterested claim to occult experience. Rilke's extraordinary gift of perception, his feeling for space which denied time or death meant that he recognized "super-natural" phenomena and events as self-evident. It is a fact that he had a lively interest in occult problems and experiments, necromancy and the like; Princess Taxis, who was a member of an international Society for Psychic Research, tells in her memoirs of several spiritualistic séances in Lautschin and Duino in which the poet had taken part: he had come into touch with the voice of an "unknown woman" who had spoken through a planchette and had received from her the strangest and most profound replies, and it was through her that he had been persuaded to travel to Toledo. This "unknown woman" had for years been one of the most important subjects they had remembered together and had been taken very seriously.

In the spring of 1921 the poet had a new and far-reaching encounter with French literature which was to bear a rich harvest. The work of Paul Valéry (1871–1945), which was small in volume but incomparable in artistic perfection, had attracted his attention and then his unreserved, even passionate admiration, and without hesitation he determined to try his hand at a translation of that great poem "Le Cimetière Marin" (published in 1920). A greater contrast could scarcely be imagined than that between Rilke and Valéry, between the poet of the "soul," of world-inwardness, and the poet of the "mind," the great Cartesian, whose theme was the hard, clear Mediterranean light. And yet a friendly, lively rapport developed between them which was one of the most splendid constellations in the literary world of the twenties. If Rilke had not been a master of his art at that time, having almost reached perfection, one would be justified in calling Valéry the last guiding star in his life. So great an inspiration was the sublime art of the Frenchman that he could consider it his salvation in his situation at that time: "I was alone, waiting, my whole work waited. One day I read Valéry; I knew that my waiting was over" (quoted by Monique Saint-Hélier in *A Rilke pour Noël.*

In addition to "Le Cimetière Marin" Rilke in course of time translated sixteen other poems by Valéry into his own language: "he was the height of splendor and, even in my best translations, I could never get near that" (to Dory von der Mühll, February 7th, 1923). To these he finally added "Eupalinos" or "On Architecture." The works that resulted in this way are indeed supreme achievements of a congenial mediator and belong to the most astonishing translations in German literature. Valéry, who did not know German, told Rilke how much he regretted that his pleasure in these works could be no more than abstract, but he reciprocated Rilke's admiration and affection. Among the many resounding names to be found in the visitors' book at Muzot, there is his also: he visited the German poet there in April 1924, and Rilke planted a willow in the garden of the castle to commemorate this great event. Their last meeting took place on September 13th, 1926, only a few months before Rilke's death, in Anthy on Lake Geneva, where they walked together for several hours in the gardens of a friend of Valéry.

In the middle of May Rilke had to leave Berg castle, which was to pass into the hands of a permanent tenant. He spent the following weeks till the end of June in Etoy across Lake Geneva where he had found a very attractive room with roses outside his window in a former Augustinian priory. In nearby Rolle he was able to meet his old Duino hostess, who helped to lift the oppression he was suffering because of certain conflicts and energetically dissuaded him from going on with his plan to publish the elegies in fragmentary form. It was the time when a new erotic relationship was entering its passionate phase: his relationship with the artist Baladine Klossowska, who after many years of travel had settled down in Geneva with her two sons Pierre and Baltusz. As early as January her call, both enticing and suppliant, had brought the poet out of his seclusion and the result was that the old distressing dilemma between "art" and "life" had to be thought over again, causing painful pangs of

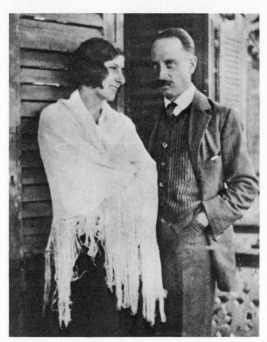

Rilke and Baladine Klossowska.

conscience, whereas to the clear-headed princess it was nothing but a superfluous burden. She wrote: "In this winter, which he needed so much, he was summoned urgently to Geneva—he had to "save" somebody again. He had to suffer because of complications and difficulties of every kind and was quite disconsolate."

It was the same Baladine of "Merline" together with whom he was travelling through Valais at the end of July when he discovered the small, massive castle tower of Muzot, situated half an hour's walk above Sierre, at some distance from the high road to Montana. Some instinct he trusted told him that here there might be a new and permanent fastness for him and his work. It was a stroke of good fortune for him that by a coincidence his Winterthur host had for a considerable time been interested in

149

the picturesque ruins and now made up his mind to rent them and place them for a time at the disposal of the poet. At the end of July after Frau Klossowska had made the house habitable, Rilke was able to move in. In a long letter to the princess, dated July 25th, 1921, he gave a masterly description of the countryside and where he was living:

"... I was imprudent enough to come down here to Sierre and Sion; I've told you what a singular magic these places exerted on me when I first saw them a year ago at the time of the grape gathering. The fact that Spain and Provence are so strangely in the landscape appealed to me in the last years before the war more powerfully and decisively than anything else; and now to find their voices united in a wide-spreading valley in Switzerland! And this echo, this family likeness is not imaginary. Only the other day I read in a treatise on the plant world of Valais that certain flowers appear here which are otherwise only to be found in Provence or Spain; it is the same with the butterflies: thus does the spirit of a great river (and for me the Rhone has always been one of the most marvelous) carry gifts and affinities through country after country. The valley is so broad here and so magnificently filled with little eminences within the frame of the great bordering mountains that it affords the eye a continual play of most bewitching modulations, like a game of chess with hills. As though hills were still being shifted about and grouped— so creative is the rhythm of what you see, an arrangement new and startling with every change of standpoint, —and the old houses and castles move all the more pleasingly in this optic game since most of them have the slope of a vineyard, the woods, the glades, or the gray rocks for a background, blended into it like the pictures on a tapestry; for a sky that is absolutely indescribable (almost rainless) has its share high up in these perspectives and animates them with so ethereal a radiance that the remarkable correlation of object to object, just as in Spain, seems to shadow forth at certain hours the tension we think we can perceive between the stars in a constellation."

With the aid of a picture postcard which shows the house as it was before additions were made in 1900, he describes Muzot: "I myself say 'castle,' for this is the perfect prototype of the sort of medieval manor that still lingers on everywhere hereabouts; these 'castles' only consist of such a single solid house-structure which comprises everything. The entrance is from the

Muzot tower.

back, where you see the sloping roof jutting out: this floor (the one with the long, built-on balcony) comprises the dining room, a small boudoir, and guest room, also the kitchen (in a modern annex) . . . On the next floor I have ensconced myself. My little bedroom is there, lighted through the window on the right, but it sends out a little balcony on the other side, straight into the tree. The double window beside it with the adjoining window in the sunny west front around the corner belongs to my study, which we more or less finished furnishing yesterday with the conveniences at hand: it has all kinds of promises and attractions for me with its old chests, its oak table of 1600, and the old dark rafters, in which the date MDCVII is engraved; when I say 'attractions' I am not being quite accurate: for actually the whole of Muzot, while it somehow holds me, nevertheless drives a sort of worry and oppression into my heart; as far as possible I have

The study at Muzot as it was in Rilke's time.

152

made myself familiar with its oldest history; the de Blonays are supposed to have built it; in the fifteenth century it was in the possession of de la Tour-Chastillon; at the beginning of the sixteenth, a year before the battle of Marignan, the marriage of Isabelle de Chevron with Jean de Montheys was celebrated here (we still know all the guests for these three days of festivity and their various goings-on). Jean de Montheys fell at Marignan and was brought back to the young widow in Muzot. Thereupon two suitors immediately burst afire for her and in their ardor came into such violent opposition that they ran one another through in a duel. The hapless Isabelle, who seemed to bear the loss of her spouse with dignity, could not get over the demise of her two swains between whom she had not yet chosen; she lost her reason and left Muzot only at night, deceiving the vigilance of her old nurse Ursule; almost every night you might see her, 'très légèrement habillée,' wandering towards Miège to the grave of her two combustible wooers, and the saying goes that finally, one winter's night, she was found in the churchyard at Miège dead and stiff. —So somehow we shall have to resign ourselves to the ghosts of Isabelle and of Jean de Montheys returning like a pendulum from Marignan, and not be surprised at anything. The Château de Muzot since we cleared it up has gained everywhere in brightness and snugness. As in all these medieval houses the rooms have something honest and peasant-like about them, rough and ready, with no reservations . . ."

The poet spent the following months almost uninterruptedly in Muzot animated by the pressing will to prepare for the return of his greatest hour, tormented by inner relapses, hesitating between confidence and profound uncertainty and contemplating often enough the necessity to abandon again his new attempt at settling somewhere as completely fruitless. He wrote the most wonderful letters to explain that he must abstain from letter writing in order to keep all his strength for his work, and his one thought remained: "to impress myself long and passionately

Rilke on the balcony at Muzot.

upon the violent and fearful breaks of the year 1914 until the skin grows over again" (to L. von Schlöter, January 21st, 1920). Towards the end of January he had to confess: "to remove the obstacles of the war years, so to speak, to remove them stone by stone from the rampart which seemed to separate me from the past as well as from everything that might have come later, is still my humble occupation, I do not know for how long" (to Lotti von Wedel, January 28th, 1922).

Scarcely five days later the spell had been broken. The great hour had come. Muzot had concealed itself in a mysterious cessation of letter writing, and behind this there was tremendous work. Just as in Duino in January 1912, where *The Life of Mary* had first to be written in order that the major work could come to life, so too it began this time with a "preliminary attack." Something quite involuntary, quite unhoped for appeared: a new, original idea and its effortless realization. Within four days, between the 2nd and 5th of February, a series of twenty-five sonnets took shape to which only one was to be added later: the first part of the *Sonnets to Orpheus* had already been conceived in an almost definitive form. But then: on the 7th the seventh elegy was written, on the 7th and 8th the eighth, which was dedicated to his friend Rudolf Kassner, on the 9th the sixth was finished and the beginnings of the ninth were taken up again and produced a radiant whole, on the 11th the tenth could be continued and concluded. On the 14th the poem which had been substituted for a fifth elegy—"Counterstrophes"—made way for one incomparably more powerful: the enchanting elegy about the travelers the subject of which had been fundamentally determined by his recollection of a famous painting by Picasso, *The Juggler* (1905). Rilke had seen it in the summer of 1915 in the Munich apartment of his Westphalian hostess Hertha König and appointed himself guardian of the Picasso for the duration of his stay there. But scarcely had the "chief business" been completed and the pain of the waiting and deprivation which had lasted for ten years been relieved by such an overpowering satisfaction than the Orphic theme reappeared and there was proof that its fruitfulness was not yet exhausted. An additional twenty-

155

nine poems were written in the days from the 15th to the 23rd of February, all achieving immaculate purity and showing no sign of declining power: the second part of the *Sonnets to Orpheus*. But that was by no means everything. In a kind of incidental activity there resulted in addition to the two cycles another series of single poems, some of which are of pre-eminent importance and would alone suffice to make this a month blessed before others: "In Merely Catching Your Own Casting," "Picture of a Vase," "To Some She Is Like Wine," and others.

All the letters he wrote during these days were couched in a deliberately "prophetic" language. The poet could do no other than proclaim this process of an unparalleled poetic emotion, this exemplary modern example of a great inspiration, with poetically radiant words, than describe it as an event of supernatural magnitude and thus make available all the material which would be used for the creation of a legend and the many hagiographies and pseudo-religious extravagances among the enormous number of books dealing with Rilke. Concepts found in the Christian religion such as "miracle" and "grace" flowed under an inner compulsion from his pen, the sruggle in art, he said, "would be hopeless without—a miracle; but art is just what it is because of that and not because of us" (to Countess Margot Sizzo-Noris-Crouy, February 19th, 1922). Was that not to formulate an aesthetic counterpart to the essence of the Christian faith and was not the poet claiming in all seriousness for himself the right to found a religion? Only by regarding the poetry as *poetry* and not as a new gospel transcending human competence can justice be done to the poet and the dangers, on the one hand, of an undue deification of Rilke (such as has been practiced in numerous books) and, on the other, of an equally misplaced Rilke-heresy hunt (such as was frequently to be noticed in recent criticism) be avoided.

World-wide fame has come to center around that simple, sturdy Valais tower of Muzot, which is today the very core of

XXIX (2. Theil)

Stiller Freund der vielen Fernen, fühle,
wie dein Atem noch den Raum vermehrt.
Im Gebälk der finstern Glockenstühle
laß dich läuten. Das, was an dir zehrt,

wird ein Starkes über dieser Nahrung.
Geh in der Verwandlung aus und ein.
Was ist deine leidendste Erfahrung?
Ist dir Trinken bitter, werde Wein.

Sei in dieser Nacht aus Übermaaß
Zauberkraft am Kreuzweg deiner Sinne,
ihrer seltsamen Begegnung Sinn.

Und wenn dich das Irdische vergaß,
zu der stillen Erde sag: Ich rinne.
Zu dem raschen Wasser sprich: Ich bin.

From the *Sonnets to Orpheus*, **XXIX**, second part.

that myth which has spread under the name of Rilke: as the symbol of an esoteric seclusion which opposes to the vacuous forms of communication of a mass society a bulwark of silence, patience, and a truly independent search for truth and language. In the opinion of the cultured public, the *Elegies* and *Sonnets* rank together with T. S. Eliot's *Waste Land,* Valéry's *Charmes,* and James Joyce's *Ulysses* as the really authoritative and formative masterpieces of the year 1922, the *annus mirabilis* of modern literature. Both cycles of poems are closely related to one another, "*Elegies* and *Sonnets* sustain each other at all points," Rilke wrote in 1925 to his Polish translator Witold Hulewicz, "and I deem it an infinite grace that I have been able, with the same breath, to swell these two sails: the little rust-colored sail of the *Sonnets* and the gigantic white canvas of the *Elegies.*" Both works express the rich range of the poet's subject matter in its final, definitive form, both present a message to the reader in the guise of poetic beauty.

Whereas the *Elegies* deal candidly with great universal issues, in the *Sonnets* there is a single legendary figure taken from Greek antiquity which the poet's imagination seized on in order to place it in the center of his thematic world as the key figure. The Thracian singer and lyre-player Orpheus: we know that Rilke was acquainted with Ovid's *Metamorphoses*, that he had already in 1904 dealt with the figure in the poem "Orpheus, Eurydice, Hermes," and that a reproduction of a pen drawing by Cima da Conegliano (circa 1459–1518) which shows the youth with his lyre surrounded by animals, hung on the wall of his study in Muzot. This Orpheus was here elevated to become the "lord" and the singing savior of a cosmos which takes in the world and the underworld, the realm of the living and that of the dead and unites them.

The singer is made into a "god" and the two decisive events of his history, his descent into the underworld and his dismemberment by the maenads, are treated as events having canonical validity and are meditated upon in a liturgical, exegetical manner, just as is the passion of Christ by Christian poets and preachers. What is this power which is elevated in Orpheus to the divine? It is the power of "celebrating," which can also appear as "song" and as "transformation" and always means just one and the same thing in all its definitions: man's capacity for feeling which finds expression through the mouth of the poet. That which in the ninth elegy is claimed for mankind as a whole, as the fundamental justification of his existence in the eyes of the angel— "*Here* is the time for the Tellable, *here* is its home./ Speak and proclaim"—, this in the *Sonnets* is given to the poet alone by a remarkably joyful and deliberate change. The poet who celebrates and transforms things appears as the representative of mankind. If, in the numerous portrayals of Orpheus in European operas from Monteverdi through Gluck to Stravinsky, the figure of the ancient singer has become the symbol of music extolling itself, in Rilke it becomes the protagonist of an apotheosis of the poet by the poet. The author of the *Sonnets* glorifies himself and his productivity and in it all the "giving" forces of the earth: the whole cycle can be understood as a thanks offering for the completion of the *Duino Elegies.*

Both works bear dedications which have been very carefully chosen and are very significant. In the case of the *Elegies* it is: "The Property of Princess Marie von Thurn und Taxis"; in the case of the *Sonnets*: "Written as a Monument for Wera Ouckama Knoop." This Wera, daughter of Gerhard and Gertrud Ouckama Knoop who belonged to the circle of Munich friends, had died at the early age of nineteen (1919), and the poet had seen her only a few times, although he had then been "singularly attracted, and moved by her," so that after her death she had become a favorite figure of his imagination as it formed myths.

"This lovely child who had just begun to dance and caused a sensation among all who saw her then by her movements and interpretation which came from some instinct in her body and

159

Wera Ouckama Knoop.

mind—, unexpectedly told her mother, that she was no longer able or desired to dance . . . ; (that was just as she was outgrowing childhood) her body changed in some strange way, and, without losing its lovely oriental configuration, became strangely heavy and massive . . . (it was the beginning of that mysterious glandular disorder which was to cause her death so soon after). . . . During her remaining time Wera played music, finally she could only draw—as if dancing which was denied her became softer and softer, more and more withdrawn . . ." (to Margot Sizzo, April 12th, 1923).

As early as January 1922 Rilke had looked after some notes on the course of the girl's illness which her mother had sent him and a compelling connection had been established between the Orphic theme and the figure of this dead girl: "whose immaturity and innocence hold open the portals of the dead so that, departed from us, she now belongs to those powers which keep the one half of life fresh and open to that other half with its wide-open wound" (to Witold Hulewicz, November 13th, 1925).

In the famous letter to Hulewicz which has already been quoted several times, Rilke tries to fit the *Elegies* meaningfully into a conspectus of his life work:

"I regard them as a further working out of those basic propositions already given in *The Book of Hours,* propositions which, in the two parts of *New Poems,* use the phenomenal world for play and experiment and finally, in *Malte,* drawn together as if in conflict, refer back to life again and almost lead to the conclusion that this life of ours, suspended as it is over a bottomless pit, is impossible. In the *Elegies* life, starting from the same data, becomes possible once more, indeed it experiences here that ultimate affirmation towards which the young Malte, although on the right and difficult road *'des longues études,'* could not yet guide it. *Affirmation of Life as well as of death prove themselves one in the Elegies."*

The meaning of Rilke's world of space in which the dimension of time is felt to have no validity is discussed: "We, the men of the present and today, we are not for one moment content in the world of time, nor are we fixed in it; we overflow continually towards the men of the Past, towards our origin and towards those who apparently come after us. In that most vast, *open* world all beings are—one cannot say 'contemporaneous,' for it is precisely the passage of Time which determines that they all *are.* This transitoriness rushes everywhere into a profound Being."

The task of man as he encounters the phenomena of this world is defined: "For such is our task: to impress this fragile and transient earth so sufferingly, so passionately upon our hearts that its essence shall rise up again, invisible, in us. *We are the bees of the Invisible* . . . The *Elegies* show us engaged in this

161

work, the work of the perpetual transformation of beloved and tangible things into the invisible vibration and excitability of our nature, which introduces new 'frequencies' into the pulsing fields of the universe. (Since the various materials in the Universe are only intensities of a spiritual kind, but, who knows? new bodies, metals, nebulae and stars.)"

Finally he explains the meaning of an angel and its superiority which is so "terrible" for us: "The angel of the *Elegies* is that Being in whom the transmutation of the Visible into the Invisible, which we seek to achieve, is consummated. For the angel of the *Elegies* all the towers and palaces of the Past are existent *because* they have long been invisible, and the still existing towers and bridges of our world *already* invisible, although still materially enduring for us. The angel of the *Elegies* is that Being who stands for the recognition in the Invisible of a higher degree of reality. That is why he is 'terrible' for us, because we, its lovers and transmuters, still cling to the Visible."

The message of the late Rilke which has only been sketched here in broad outline is closely related to the most significant events, developments, and portents of recent thought; there are many similarities and reminders. Some things refer back to Nietzsche: the anti-Christian passion, the rejection of the "Beyond," the jubilant "life here's glorious" of the seventh elegy, which must be taken in conjunction with "Earth, you darling, I will" in the ninth if one is correctly to appreciate its distinctive pitch, its mood which is "Franciscan" rather than "Dionysian." Some things point forward to Heidegger who, taking a single poem, gave in his *Holzwege* (1950) one of the most beautiful and profound interpretations of Rilke which we possess. The whole is a spiritual and artistic event of independent magnitude: it imagines a world, determines a situation, and creates a style in a way almost unparalleled in his time. This poetic world of a homeless man who created a home for himself,

162

so to speak, out of nothing by setting alight his feeelings, by "inwardness," as he called it, this world has since become a spiritual home for innumerable readers. Wild enthusiasm, critical antipathy, and inexhaustible interpretative frenzy have now been fighting over this work for more than three decades. Many have claimed to find in the teaching of the *Elegies* and the *Sonnets* something like a new religion of life; others have attacked it from religious, philosophical, political, and ideological stand-points. However, the work of art as a form has a truth of its own which can indeed be called in question by critical arguments but never demolished. By the revolutionary power of his language and the compelling individuality of his ideas Rilke has opened up a new and wide horizon of possible perception enabling man to seek his real *raison d'être* in a historical context of feeling.

THE LAST YEARS

The poet still had four years to live when he had finished the most difficult task of his life. He spent the greater part of this time at Muzot, the seclusion and incredible quiet of which was still to be favorable for some productive work. Werner Reinhart had purchased the tower in May 1922 and had, generously and definitively, invested his guest once more with it.

With the end of that first winter in Valais, the ice of his most rigorous solitude was broken for Rilke. He felt more active again, in a mood for travel and ready for the pleasure and adventure of meeting people. After having been in Muzot for a year and a half he felt sometimes that the isolation of his secluded house was a hindrance and occasionally complained about "having become curiously dulled as regards this landscape whose marvels

I have felt so deeply, yet I have to hold them before my eyes with an effort, deliberately, if I am still to partake of them" (to Lou, January 13th, 1923).

In summer and autumn he was often away, sometimes in the German speaking part of Switzerland, sometimes in the other parts; he liked especially to go to the Wunderly's house in Meilen on Lake Zurich, which he had first visited in 1920. At the end of that year poor health forced him to go for the first time to the sanatorium of Valmont sur Territet on Lake Geneva. He remained till January 20th, then returned to his tower and was soon absorbed again in work.

During the following summer also he was absent for a long time, traveling by car with Frau Wunderly through the French speaking part of Switzerland, and spending some weeks in Ragaz spa (in the canton of Sankt Callen) with the princess, seeking to recover his health. Towards the end of the year, on November 24th, he was back again in Valmont where he remained until January 8th, and from there he went, feeling tolerably well, to make a prolonged stay in Paris. France and its world of books was once more right in the foreground of his literary interests after he had renewed those ties which had been broken by the war, and his library in Muzot consisted largely of French publications that had appeared in the twenties. Paris responded most cordially to his warmth of feeling: when he arrived he was the center of acclamation, and a wave of respect and curiosity pressed towards him. Everybody wanted to talk to him or invite him, women belonging to fashionable society were constantly telephoning him, men of the greatest distinction like Charles du Bos, Edmond Jaloux, André Gide sought his friendship or renewed acquaintance. Two cases of valuable personal belongings which Rilke had had to leave behind in Paris in 1914 were returned to him. Gide had rescued them and stored them in the cellers of the Librairie Gallimard, publishers of the *Nouvelle Revue Française.*

In Paris, 1925.

Quite contrary to his former custom Rilke allowed himself to be made the center of a social season. He was frequently together with Baladine Klossowska who had meanwhile left Geneva to go and live in Paris. In the mornings he worked with Maurice Betz, a poet of the younger generation (1898–1946), at the latter's translation of *Malte,* enjoying the fine shades of meaning in the two languages with which he was most familiar and the admiration of the gifted and charming man sitting opposite him. Betz was also the editor of *Reconnaissance à Rilke,* which came out in 1926 as a double number of the *Cahiers du Mois* with contributions by Paul Valéry, Edmond Jaloux, Jean Cassou, Daniel-Rops, and many other French and non-French authors; he also wrote that splendid book of reminiscences *Rilke Vivant*, which appeared in 1937. It was the old Paris where life was lived with the greatest intensity imaginable and yet in other respects was not.

On August 18th, after repeatedly postponing his departure, Rilke left the city quite abruptly and without saying a word, traveled to Burgundy with Frau Klossowska, spending two days in Dijon, then through Sierre to Lake Maggiore and Milan, finally reaching Ragaz at the end of September after passing through Muzot; he was then traveling alone to undergo "belated, too late treatment." Had he only been driven away by too much social life, was he just weary after being with so many people and longing to be alone?

"No, this ailment, this indisposition by which I was suddenly attacked in Paris, was very bad and difficult to explain; I was wearied by my oldest and best friends, and indeed even by friendship itself which suddenly became an effort beyond my strength. I was no longer up to it, I did not desire it, I who, after becoming aware to some extent of the powers of my heart and brain, knew of no more delightful pleasure than to devote myself to those whose contact and real presence I could feel."

The lyric output of these last four years followed the enthusiastic years of 1922 like a gentle, pensive coda following a heroic allegro. A great cyclic idea was no longer possible; those impulses which united so strongly to produce the *Elegies* and the *Sonnets* appear now only in isolation. The hour of the "thing poem" could not be repeated. The poet did find once again a new tone, a new, one might almost say, "lyric" world concept, and reasons worthy of attention have been adduced to prove that the works dating from 1924 and 1925 even surpass the *Elegies* in poetic maturity, and that it was only in the corpus of these last poems which no longer contain a doctrine or a message that Rilke reached the highest stage of his development. They were short rhyming nature poems, creating a mood or recalling something from the past, concentrated and fragrant after the manner of a song, sometimes with two stanzas but mostly with three, tender and precise. Rilke celebrates the Valais countryside without whose great, silent help his main work would not have been completed, and sees in its details the equivalent of his own state of mind.

But this phase of Rilke's creative work cannot be characterized in a few sentences either. Its substance is inexhaustible. In addition to the poems inspired by his walks, expressing the moods of the landscape, the vineyards, gardens, mountain meadows, there are certain lyric meditations surpassing in profundity anything yet written, as, for example, the dedicatory poem "As Nature Lets the Other Creatures Follow" (June 14th, 1924), which has been interpreted by Heidegger, or the equally excellent "The Swing Swept into Pain and Back Again" (1923/1924): they seem to have penetrated to the heart of the mystery of human existence. In other texts again—"Idol," "Arrival," "Gong"— one almost has the impression that the extremely delicate language of the poet is, as it were, about to change into the language of birds or fish, no longer or not yet audible to human ears. What have become best known are a group of poems which are, so to speak, at the center of success: in which the central motifs of the world as Rilke understood it are again put forward and new proofs supplied of the creative genius of the human heart. "The Horn of Plenty" (written for Hugo von Hofmannsthal), "The Magician," "Tear Vase," "Since Soaring Rapture," "Mutability," "Gods Perhaps Stride," "Full Power," and others, as well as the two sets of poems "Drafts from Two Winter Evenings" (for Anton Kippenberg) and "Written in the Churchyard of Ragaz" (June 1924). These latest products of Rilke's genius are distinguished by a conciseness of expression, a firmness of structure in the line and the stanza and a power of moderation

167

and simplicity which are a new artistic victory over himself, as a final triumph over certain extravagances of earlier phases, excesses of virtuosity and exaggerations of chromatic style.

And, finally, it is to these years that almost the whole opus of the poems written in French belongs. The titles of the individual collections indicate their character: *Verges, Les Roses, Les Fenêtres, Quatrains Valsains.* They are short poems, mostly of two or three stanzas, depicting a landscape and suggesting a mood, in honor of that grand and inexhaustible natural scenery surrounding him, and tributes to the sister language which he used throughout his life with such pleasure and gratitude. None of them is quite as successful as the German counterparts, but equally none is without that linguistic *esprit de finesse* which Rilke's sensorial gifts had acquired during the decades.

After an unsuccessful course of treatment in Ragaz in September 1925 Rilke went back to Muzot by way of Meilen. He did not feel well, wrote that he was a broken man, complained of constant pain, and considered his illness was more serious than the doctors had diagnosed. "Muzot," he wrote to the princess, "often seems to me difficult and lonely in this anxious time, and yet, how glad I am to have this refuge; as soon as my doctor has returned to Valmont I shall once more have to exchange my seclusion and freedom for the sanatorium which for two years now has been a kind of annex to Muzot" (December 11th, 1925).

In the middle of the month he was back in the care of Dr. Haemmerlis and remained until the end of May 1926. He spent a large part of the summer again in Ragaz where he met the princess for the last time. After some happy days on Lake Geneva and that meeting with Valéry which has already been mentioned, he returned to Sierre but did not go to Muzot, staying instead in a room at the Hotel Bellevue for two months. On November 30th he had to return to Valmont once again, seriously ill this

Rarogne church.

time and facing death. At last the nature of his illness had been established: a rare form of leukemia.

He wrote to Nanny Wunderly on December 8th: "Day and night, day and night . . . hell! I know what it is! What is most difficult and protracted is resignation, to accept that one is an 'invalid.' A sick dog is still a dog. But we, are we still ourselves after a certain degree of senseless pain?"

Of all his friends only one was near him during these days, Nanny Wunderly-Volkart. According to J. R. von Salis, who has written a biography about his years in Switzerland, he is supposed to have said to her: "Help me to *my* death!" It is said, by the way, that the word "hell" was often used, the word "death" hardly ever: as if he were reluctant to recognize that this terrible affliction was identical with what he had glorified at first in *The Book of Hours* and then repeatedly till the end as his "own death." It was on December 29th, three and a half hours after midnight, that the end came—a peaceful end after twelve hours' sleep: his head rose once more with his eyes wide open and then sank back on to the pillows. The man who seemed to embody like no other before or after him the concept of "pure poet" had passed away.

In his will, which he had made on October 27th, 1925, and put into Frau Wunderly's hands—*fidèles entre toutes*—, there were precise instructions about where he wanted to be buried: ". . . I should prefer to be interred in the churchyard up near the old church of Rarogne. Its enclosure is one of the first places where I experienced the wind and the light of this countryside."

On January 2, 1927, Rainer Maria Rilke was carried to his grave in this very place, just within the German linguistic frontier and scarcely half an hour's distance by car up the Rhône from Muzot. The epitaph which he himself composed runs as follows:

> Rose, oh the pure contradiction. Delight,
> of being no one's sleep under so many
> lids

During his lifetime the rose, this ancient Western symbol of the *unio mystica,* was for Rilke a source of rapture and meditative devotion. Here it now becomes the metaphor for the "pure," that is, for the contradiction that has been resolved and accepted into man's own will as a law of his life. As "no man's sleep under so many lids," as abundance growing from nothingness, it becomes the flower that is symbolic of the meaning of the world. At the same time it is here a cipher for the being of the dead

170

View of the Rhône valley from the churchyard of Rarogne.

poet: the German *"Lider"* is ambiguous and means not only "eye lids" but also the songs left to us by the genius of the poet. Behind them, behind the full, radiant, fragrant flowers of his work, he himself, the author of this incomparable epitaph, disappears, a nothingness, a sleep that no one is sleeping.

Rainer Maria Rilke

171

CHRONOLOGICAL TABLE

1875	December 4th, Rilke born in Prague.
1882–1884	Attends the Piarists' school in Prague.
1886–1890	Enters Junior Military School at Sankt Pölten.
1890–1891	Enters Senior Military School at Mährisch-Weiss-kirchen.
1891–1892	Studies at the School of Commerce at Linz.
1892–1895	Prepares for the final secondary school examination in Prague.
1894	Publishes his first book, *Life and Songs*.
1895	Begins university studies in Prague.
1896–1897	Two university terms in Munich. Moves to Berlin.
1898	Spring journey to Italy.
1899	Berlin and Prague. April–June: first journey to Russia.
1900	May–June: second journey to Russia. Visits Heinrich Vogeler in Worpswede. Meets Clara Westhoff.
1901	Marries Clara and lives in Westerwede near Bremen. December 12th: Ruth Rilke is born.
1902	August: Arrives in Paris. Studies Rodin.
1903	Journey to Italy.
1904	June–December: journey to Sweden instigated by Ellen Key.
1905	January–May: in Worpswede. June: visits Lou Andreas-Salomé in Göttingen. In Berlin, Kassel, Marburg before returning to Paris. October in Dresden and Prague. Christmas in Worpswede.
1906	Father dies. Journey to France and Belgium.
1906–1908	Frequent journeys to Capri. Lecture tours through Germany and Austria.
1909	In France.
1910	In Leipzig early in the year to visit his publisher Kippenberg. April in Duino. August, guest of Princess Marie von Thurn und Taxis at the castle of Lautschin.

1911	In Egypt. Returns through Italy to Paris. Journeys through Germany.
1912	Till the beginning of May in Duino. Venice.
1912–1913	October–February: journey through Spain.
1913	Stays in Paris, Göttingen, Leipzig, Weimar, Berlin, Munich, Dresden.
1914	Further journeys, then from August in Munich.
1915	Army medical examination.
1916	Military service in Vienna at records office. June, discharge and return to Munich.
1919	June 11th, departure for Switzerland.
1920	Journey to Venice. November, living in the castle of Berg in Irchel.
1921	Werner Reinhart rents the Château de Muzot and offers it to the poet as residence.
1922	Finishes the *Duino Elegies* and the *Sonnets to Orpheus*.
1923	December in the sanatorium of Valmont.
1924	Further treatment in the sanatorium of Valmont.
1925	January–February in Paris. From October in Muzot. From December in Valmont.
1926	Returns for the summer to Muzot. From November 30th in Valmont. December 29th, Rilke dies.
1927	January 2nd, buried at Rarogne (Valais).

BIBLIOGRAPHY

1. Works

The Book of Hours. A. L. Peck, trans. London, 1961.

Duino Elegies. J. B. Leishman and S. Spender, trans. London, 1957.

Ewald Tragy. New York.

From Remains of C. W. New York, 1952.

The Lay of the Love and Death of Cornet Christopher Rilke. M. H. Norton, trans. New York, 1959.

Letters of Rainer Maria Rilke, Vol. 1: 1892–1910; Vol. 2: 1901–1926. New York, 1969.

Letters of Rainer Maria Rilke and Princess Marie von Thurn und Taxis. New York, 1958.

Letters to a Young Poet. M. H. Norton, trans. New York, 1954.

Letters to Frau Gudi-Nolke During His Life in Switzerland. New York, 1955.

New Poems. J. B. Leishman, trans. New York, 1964.

Notebooks of Malte Laurids Brigge. M. H. Norton, trans. New York, 1964.

Poems from the Book of Hours. B. Deutsch, trans. New York, 1968.

Poems, 1906–1926. J. B. Leishman, trans. New York.

Requiem. New York.

Selected Letters of R. M. Rilke, 1902–1926. R. F. C. Hull, trans. London, 1947.

Selected Poems. C. G. MacIntyre, trans. Berkeley, Calif., 1941.

Selected Works. Vol. 1: Prose. G. C. Houston, trans. *Vol. 2: Poetry.* J. B. Leishman, trans. New York, 1960.

Sonnets to Orpheus. M. H. Norton, trans. New York, 1942.

Stories of God. M. H. Norton, trans. New York, 1963.

Translations from the Poetry of Rainer Maria Rilke. M. H. Norton, trans. New York, 1962.

Wartime Letters of Rainer Maria Rilke, 1914–1921. New York, 1940.

2. Biography and Criticism

BATTERBY, K. A. J. *Rilke and France: A Study in Poetic Development.* New York, 1966.

BELMORE, H. W. *Rilke's Craftsmanship.* New York, 1955.

FUERST, NORBERT. *Phases of Rilke.* New York, 1958.

GRAY, RONALD. *German Tradition in Literature, 1871–1945.* New York, 1966.

GUARDINI, ROMANO. *Rilke's Duino Elegies: An Interpretation.* Chicago, 1961.

HARTMAN, GEOFFREY H. *Unmediated Vision.* New York, 1966.

MANDEL, SIEGFRIED. *Rainer Maria Rilke: The Poetic Instinct.* Carbondale, Ill., 1965.

MASON, EUDO C. *Rilke, Europe, and the English-Speaking World.* New York, 1961.

PETERS, H. FREDERICK. *Rainer Maria Rilke: Masks and the Man.* Seattle, 1960.

SALIS, J. R. VON. *Rainer Maria Rilke: The Years in Switzerland.* N. K. Cruickshank, trans. Berkeley, Calif., 1964.

SHAW, PRISCILLA. *Rilke, Valéry and Yeats: The Domain of the Self.* New Brunswick, N.J., 1964.